"*Broken and Beautiful* is powerful, passionate, and full of divine purpose. You will never look at life the same after reading it."

—Lady Brigitte Gabriel, founder and chairwoman, ACT for America; New York Times bestselling author

"*Christine Soule shares her life story with positive courage, even the most painful and heartbreaking moments. Her contagious joy in revealing the loving Savior who intercedes in her life, in both good and bad moments, fills the pages with surprises and promise.*"

—Carrie Abbott, president, The Legacy Institute; host, Relationship Insights Radio

"*As you will read in Broken and Beautiful, my friend Christine Soule has "a Jericho anointing." The power God has given her by grace allows her to break down people's walls of fear and insecurity and woundedness and shame. Be prepared to cry. Expect to be broken. But also know that golden wisdom and love will flow into your broken places as you keep reading. When you finish—or better, when God gets finished with you—you will be more beautiful than you ever thought you could be.*"

—Joseph Castleberry, Ed.D. President, Northwest University

D1527594

BROKEN
and
BEAUTIFUL

Let God Turn Your Mess into a Masterpiece

BY CHRISTINE SOULE

CONTENTS

I dedicate this book to my beloved husband, Mitch Soule. I feel so blessed, honored, and deeply humbled that I get to do this life with you. You, my love, have taught me to believe in myself, to know the Lord at a greater depth, and to fiercely follow my dreams!

Your generosity and servanthood in everything you do is an example to everyone around you. Thank you for being the man of God that you are. For being my husband and best friend. For tolerating me in all my crazy adventures, and for your patience as I pursue the things I believe God has called me to do. Thank you for being the most amazing father to our children that I could ever hope for or dream of.

And thank you for being the best chef and cookie maker around!

I await with anticipation what the future holds for this beautiful life we get to live! Buckle your seat belt. It's going to be an amazing ride!

PREFACE

I sat down with my friend Akhtar Badshah, formerly head of Microsoft Philanthropies, to seek his advice about launching a new Christian nonprofit organization called Providence Heights. Providence Heights will empower women in need through housing, employment opportunities, and personal development programs rooted in Christian faith while reinvesting revenues generated through real-estate enterprises. Our vision is for every individual to have a home and to thrive in pursuit of God's purpose for them.

Akhtar told me three things that I will never forget.

"First off," he said, "you're totally unrealistic." He paused and then repeated, "You are completely unrealistic."

My heart sank because everybody else had been so positive about what we were doing.

He continued, "You know, how unrealistic is it that a poor boy from India could get an MIT scholarship and later become the professor? And then become the head of Microsoft Philanthropies? Totally unrealistic, isn't it? Be unrealistic."

"The second thing that comes to my mind is that you're going to fail. You are going to fail, big time. The difference between you and about 80 percent of the world is that you're going to get back up. So get back up."

The third thing he said to me was, "You are totally and completely unqualified."

I threw my hands in the air, laughed, and said, "I know!"

"Be unqualified," he said. "Qualified people have two problems. First, they think they know everything, and they don't need to know more. They stop growing as a result. Second, they think they don't need anyone because they've got all the answers for themselves. But unqualified people never want to stop learning, and they bring people around them with great wisdom so that they can work together as a team. Be unqualified."

We all come in with insecurities. Feeling that we aren't qualified. We aren't capable.

We're going to fail. The truth is, that's exactly where God wants us to be so that He can grow us. It's okay to feel broken and lost. But what do we do with that? Discover who we are in Christ. God's Word says that it is He who qualifies you. If you're feeling like you are out of your element, congratulations! You're exactly where you need to be. Most of us face our journeys with at least some insecurity, afraid we'll fail.

Akhtar was right, of course; it is to our advantage to embrace being unqualified, so we'll keep learning and growing. And I've taken that advice to heart as I begin this venture. But I also know something more about being unqualified: that's exactly where God wants us to be because He wants us to learn and grow *with Him as our guide.*

Even better, at the same time, God offers us His qualification. In 2 Corinthians 3:5, the apostle Paul wrote, "It is not that we think we are qualified to do anything on our own. Our qualification comes from God."

So if you're feeling insecure and unqualified about anything at all as you begin reading this book, congratulations! You're exactly where you need to be. Just don't forget you can access God's qualification as you move forward.

The key is discovering who you are in Christ—your *true* identity. And that's especially significant if you, like me, have a past of brokenness. Some of you are probably living with brokenness now. But as I've processed through my own journey, much of it told in these pages through the trajectory of my life so far, I've realized just how many women struggle with their identity, with who they are and what their purpose is. So much of how we see ourselves revolves around the demands our society places on us, insisting we live up to its expectations.

Don't listen to the world. Listen to God.

The world says, "Your brokenness defines you." But God says, "Beloved, *I* define you. Nothing else."

The world says, "If you've gone through trauma or abuse, you're stuck. You'll struggle the rest of your life with anxiety, depression, and so many obstacles to overcome." Yet God's Word says, "You will keep in perfect peace all who trust in you, all whose thoughts are fixed on you!" (Isaiah 26:3).

God's Word is true and real. He has a completely different plan for us, and when He says perfect peace, He means perfect peace! He's bigger than any life circumstances, powerful to heal and restore. He intends for our identity as women to come from Him and Him alone.

That's why I've written this book for the broken, all of whom need God to mend them.

INTRODUCTION

God's Gold

Kintsugi[1] is an ancient Japanese art form I've practiced myself. The word is Japanese for "golden joinery." According to its background story, a Japanese military commander broke one of his valued Chinese tea bowls and sent the pieces to China for repair. But when the bowl was returned, the pieces had merely been joined together with unsightly staples.

This time the commander gave it to a Japanese artist, who separated the pieces, then glued them back together before filling each crack with gold. Instead of trying to hide the broken lines, the artist highlighted them, transforming the bowl's shattered pieces into the source of its greatest value. Rather than the bowl becoming worthless and being thrown away, its broken places became the places it was strongest. It became even more precious and valuable.

When I first gazed at an image of Kintsugi art, the practice so resonated with my spirit. As you'll soon read,

---

1   Nerdwriter, "Kintsugi: The Art of Embracing Damage," May 30, 2014, YouTube video, https://www.youtube.com/watch?v=IT55_u8URU0.

I once felt completely shattered. But then the experiences that broke me led to a greater beauty in me.

So often we reject our broken places or hide from them. We pretend what broke us didn't happen. We place blame or anger on those who shattered us. Worse, we let our brokenness define us. But instead of being defined by our brokenness, we can be defined by the beauty that God, the ultimate artist, creates in us with His gold.

Let me tell you the amazing story of a broken girl who found that gold.

God's Gold Applied

A high school girl I'll call Rachel was being raised by her grandmother and aunt. Sadly, she was merely tolerated most of the time, but worse, sometimes she was beaten. Yet she was grateful for a place to live and food on the table.

A straight-A student, Rachel decided to apply to some colleges. She asked her aunt to help her with the process, but when the woman said, "I'm not your mother, nor do I choose to be," Rachel reached a turning point. Feeling hopeless, she stopped participating in school, not even turning in her assignments. Her grades rapidly fell to the point her principal called her grandmother.

"I don't know what's going on," the principal told her, "but Rachel isn't applying herself anymore."

When Rachel came home from school, her grandmother beat her with a household object—and with a vengeance. Rachel thought, *I've been beaten before, but never like this.* She was confident she would die that day. But when the object her grandmother used broke, the woman walked away to find another weapon, allowing Rachel time to run to the bathroom and lock the door.

Desperate, she grabbed a container of bleach and prepared to drink it in hopes she could end her life before her grandmother did.

But then her phone buzzed with a text from a girl at her school. It read, "Whatever you're about to do, please don't do it."

Rachel was astonished. She didn't really know this classmate. They'd done some school assignments together, but they had no real relationship.

Still stunned, Rachel called her, and in desperation, she relayed the danger she was in and how hopeless she felt. "But how did you know?" she asked.

"My parents and I knew someone was going to need a home and our love, and so we prepared a room. Then we began to pray, and now we know you're the one. Please do whatever you need to do to get out of that house. You're welcome here, and you have a home with us."

Rachel packed her belongings and left as fast as she could. The girl took her to church the following Sunday, and here's where my hero friend Jeanne comes in.

Jeanne runs an intern program for teens and college students at that church. At the end of the service, she asked to speak to Rachel and invited the girls to her office. Jeanne knew brokenness from her own life experiences and, as a result, was gifted with great empathy and compassion. She lifted Rachel's hand and touched one of the bruises on her arm. "I'm so sorry," she told her. Then she touched another bruise and said, "I'm so, so sorry." She continued doing that, then gave Rachel a hug and said over and over, "I love you."

"This is the first time in my entire life anyone has said they love me," Rachel said.

But Jeanne had more to offer. "I want you to join our intern program."

"But I'm Muslim."

"I don't care. I want you to join."

Six months into the program, Rachel gave her life to the Lord, and the cracks in her life filled with the gold only He can provide. Her brokenness was made beautiful.

Our brokenness is often like that. The worst parts of our story can bring the best parts in our lives. And that's what I hope you learn in these pages. I use my story to illustrate the power of God to turn the cracks of life to gold, but this book isn't about me. It's about you.

God Speaks to Us

Throughout this book, I write a lot about how God speaks to me. So before we move into the first chapter, I want to touch on how we can all hear His voice.

Many people don't believe God speaks, but He spoke the world into existence, and He's still speaking. He's never stopped! Scripture says, "Jesus Christ is the same yesterday, today, and forever" (Hebrews 13:8), so we know the God of Genesis is the God of today. He spoke to His people, to prophets, and to kings, and today He still speaks through His Word, through others, and certainly through the Holy Spirit.

Jesus told us He sent the Holy Spirit to be our helper, to guide and direct us. What a beautiful gift the Holy Spirit is! To forget about the Holy Spirit would be like going to a grocery store and buying all your food, only to get home and realize the meat and the ice cream aren't there. You paid for them, but you left them at the register. So what are you going to do about that? You're going to go back to the store and get your ice cream and steak. They're already bought. They're yours to claim.

Jesus paid the price for our salvation, and we can all accept that gift from our Savior. But just as on the cross Jesus bought us freedom from sin, shame, pain, and sickness, He's also given us the gift of the

Holy Spirit. This gift—this Helper from God who speaks to us—is ours to receive. I trust you'll discover why He's so vital to our walk with God as you read this book.

CHAPTER 1

OVERCOME YOUR FEARS

My arm shook as I pressed the phone receiver against my ear. I was nine and alone in the house.

"I know where you are," a strange man's voice said from the other end. I froze. I couldn't think of a word to say. "You know how I know?" he continued. "I was just in the house with you."

I don't remember most of my childhood, but I do remember the terrifying phone calls I got when I was in fourth grade.

My mom worked during the day, and my stepfather wasn't home either, so when I got pneumonia and couldn't go to school, I was alone, watching cartoons in my jammies on the couch. I was in the middle of an episode of *She-Ra* when the first call came.

I won't recount the specifics of what I was told, but it was a rape threat, and the man on the other end of the line described what he was going to do to me in graphic detail. Then he told me what my house looked like on the inside before describing what I was wearing and telling me he knew because he'd been in my house watching me.

By the time the call ended, I was not only paralyzed with fear but too frightened to tell my mother.

The next day he called again. Same threats. Same scary revelation. "You know how I know all this? I was in the house with you."

The calls kept coming, day after day. Terrified, I looked for him under every bed, behind every door and every curtain. I could never find him, but I was sure he was there, watching me. Rape and death lurked just moments away.

Finally, I gathered enough courage to report the phone calls to my mom.

Now, let me stop a moment to tell you about my parents and siblings.

My dad was an alcoholic, and Mom left him when I was five. He'd been married seven times before he married her. I think I met fifteen half-siblings at his funeral even though his deal was that when he divorced, he divorced the whole family, never to see them again. But we were his last family, and he elected to raise my two brothers. I grew up with my mom, and my sister bounced back and forth between her and my dad.

My mom was a hero. She survived three horrific marriages, and sometimes she worked three jobs, doing her best to love and care for me. But you could count on one hand how many times I saw my dad after Mom left him. He just didn't know how to be a good father, at least not to me. I was the kid on the doorstep waiting for the car that never pulled up. He'd say, "I'll come get you for the weekend," but it wouldn't happen. Just broken promises.

Mom's next marriage was to a man I'll call Scott, my stepdad when the calls came, and that takes us back to my story.

When I finally told Mom about the calls, she contacted the police. I guess she didn't tell Scott, though, because when they tapped our phone, they discovered he was the caller! I thought, *Are you kidding me? Scott is supposed to be my dad!* Turned out he was a convicted rapist. When he met Mom, he had just been released from prison, incarcerated after raping his two-year-old daughter.

Thankfully, Scott returned to prison for three years, and Mom divorced him while he was there. But when I was in junior high, he was released and came back to haunt us. Mom's bedroom window was on the second floor, but mine was on the ground level. He would park his car and then pace outside my window to torment me. He never came inside, but still I was petrified.

Eventually he stopped coming. So once the threat disappeared, my fear should have disappeared too, right?

If only.

Just coming home alone after school terrified me. Every time I walked in the front door, I had to make sure I was safe. I looked behind every door. Behind the drapes. Inside the closets. Everywhere. The shower curtain always had to be left open, but I checked the tub just to make sure no one was hiding there.

When I dropped out of high school (more about that later), we lived in a small apartment on the top floor of a three-story building. We had decent neighbors, but one day we discovered an attic opening that connected to their attics, meaning any one of them could sneak into our house. We had no way to keep them out. I couldn't sleep after that, and we couldn't move away fast enough!

I just couldn't shake the feeling that someone was out to get me. I was still being stalked, only this time the stalker wasn't my stepdad. My stalker was fear itself.

Living with Fear

That spirit of fear, gripping me to the core, followed me into my adult life. Even after I had come to know Jesus and married Mitch—the love of my life, the man of my dreams, my best friend ever, and the safest guy in the world—fear was always there.

If Mitch went on a business trip, I wouldn't sleep the whole time he was gone. My kids would celebrate getting to stay in our room, but I was afraid something might happen to them. I'd leave the light on in the hallway so I could see the sliver of light shining under the closed door of my bedroom, watching it all night to make sure no shadows passed across it. Fear ruled my life. I told myself over and over, *You'll be okay. Your house is safe; no one's going to harm you.* But I still couldn't shake the fear.

Sometimes hairline fractures sink deep and aren't easily repaired. All the logic in the world couldn't help me. Do you ever feel like you know that what you're feeling doesn't make any sense, that it's not logical, but it's still there no matter how hard you fight against it? It doesn't matter how many times you tell yourself, *This is nuts; you're fine.* A still, small voice whispers, "But what if you're not fine?"

We're so moldable in our youth, and hopefully our fathers make us feel safe. But early on I learned I wasn't safe from the man who was supposed to be my father. That was my reality. Someone was always out to get me. Looking back now, I can tell myself, *He was crazy. He ended up in jail for molesting his own daughter.* But when you're a kid, you have no such filter. You have no way to process what you're going through and no logical voice to counter threats. You just feel fear.

And fear took its mallet and hammered a fracture across my heart.

But when I met my heavenly Father, He taught me a new reality. And just like with Kintsugi art, the artist, God, highlighted the cracks Scott caused in my life, bringing out a greater beauty in me with His gold.

The Breakthrough

My fight against fear took a turn when I went on a business trip to LA with Mitch. He attended a convention during the day, and in the evenings we just hung out at our hotel in Beverly Hills.

Then one night he came back super excited.

"I have this amazing surprise for you," he said. (The surprise isn't relevant to this story, but it *was* amazing!) "I can tell you only one part of it, though. We're switching hotels! The only problem is, you have to be out of this hotel at noon tomorrow, and I can't be back until four o'clock. So I'll leave the car with you, and then you can shop around in LA before picking me up at the Staples Center."

He was super stoked, but I thought, *I'm going to die. I'm dead. He doesn't understand. I'm dead.* I was terrified I would die alone in LA sometime during those four hours.

He left the next morning giddy as could be, but I was still traumatized. I got in the shower, where I do some of my best praying, probably a development rooted in being a mother to so many kids. Showering was the only time I could find any stinking silence in my house! But I can tell you, this was not a silent shower. I didn't just pray; I cried. And I cried out to God.

Now, I was a pretty new believer, so I hadn't yet memorized much Scripture, and I didn't really know what God promises us regarding peace. I just knew I was terrified and didn't want to die. So, alone in a strange city, with nowhere to go and no one else to depend on, I went to God.

Thankfully, I did remember one verse: "If God is for us, who can ever be against us?" (Romans 8:31). Suddenly, I felt the most amazing, supernatural peace. It was the weirdest thing, as though a fog had lifted. I could see I was going to be fine. But I *felt* fine too.

Okay, let's do this.

I finished getting ready, then packed our stuff and checked out of the hotel, deciding to drive toward the Staples Center in downtown LA first so I could get my bearings. Then I'd figure out what to do for the next four hours. But I also wanted to grab some lunch, so I pulled into the parking lot of a well-known fast-food restaurant, got out of the car, and walked inside.

The place was unlike any fast-food place I'd ever seen. All the chairs and tables were bolted to the floor, like a picnic table at a park is bolted to a concrete slab so it can't be moved or stolen. Weirder still, there were no workers. No one to take my order.

So I headed back out the door, and on my way to my car, I spotted a narrow brick building off to the side. I walked up to it and found a window with thick, bulletproof glass, a place where you could order. The window had a little space at the bottom that slid open and shut.

I was so confused.

The guy at the window immediately said, "Honey, you're in gang territory, and you need to get out of here *now!*"

But his words didn't faze me. I had total peace. So I said, "Hmm, I'd like a cheeseburger with fries. No lettuce or ketchup, please."

Then I heard steps behind me. When I turned, I found three young men, one of them with a knife in his hand. None of them spoke to me, but as I finished placing my order and then stood aside to wait for my food, the one with the knife kept flipping it up in the air and catching it, flipping it and catching it, over and over.

Yep, I was still totally at peace. Zero fear, guys!

When I got my food, I headed to my car. But then I noticed an outside table and thought, *Oh. Well, I'm just going to sit down and eat here.*

The men followed me to the table, and then one sat on my right and another sat on my left. The guy with the knife stood behind me, and I could hear him continuing to flip his knife and catch it, flip it and catch it, flip it and catch it.

Then their silence ended, they took turns telling me what they were going to do to me, and I kid you not, they made almost exactly the same threats my stepfather made to me over the phone in fourth grade. But this time God's peace covered me.

Deciding to engage them, I looked at the one on my right and said, "What's your name?" But he just kept threatening me.

Without acknowledging those threats, I turned to the guy on the other side of me. "So are you from here?" I asked him. But I just got more threats from him as well.

I know it's amazing, but I really wasn't bothered by their threats. I understood they were people just like me, with hopes and needs, and I refused to see them as anything else. I refused to give in to fear.

Once one of them finally gave me the dignity of a response to one of my questions, it must have clicked for them all that I was a human too. By the time I was finished eating, they were all sitting down, and I was showing them photos of my children.

"What do you guys want to do with your lives?" I finally asked.

One of them replied, "I just want to take out the other guy before he can take me out."

"What do you mean?"

"What I said. I'm just going to take out the other guy before he has a chance to take me out."

"No, I'm serious," I told him.

"I'm serious too."

"Well, don't you want to accomplish something with your life?"

We all went back and forth on that question for about ten minutes. I kept praying for an answer that held a bigger dream, but they just couldn't entertain the thought of anything more than survival.

This is the place so many young people live. They just want to survive. But kids who can't dream become adults with no vision. And without a vision, the people perish (Proverbs 29:18).

As we continued talking, though, they started opening up. One guy confessed he'd actually killed someone, describing how it felt, saying he'd been merely protecting himself but regretted it afterward. They told me about their grandmas, their moms, and other people important in their lives. We talked about the threats they lived with every day. Imagine that—the very fear they threatened me with was the same fear they experienced daily. And now here I was trying to help them walk through their fear.

Wow, God's so good!

When I got up to leave, they insisted on walking me to my car. I joyfully let them, knowing they wanted to protect me from harm.

One of them said to the others, "She's phat."

I spun around. "I'm what?"

"You're phat!"

"You're calling me fat?" I laughed.

"No, phat's good! Like, 'You're bad,'" he said, trying to explain the slang.

"Okay, so now I'm bad." I couldn't resist.

I laughed again as they kept trying to express their respect for me in terms with definitions opposite of the definitions I knew. It was hilarious but beautiful too. The next time they encountered a woman, I'm sure they looked at her a little differently.

I know that afternoon transformed those three men, but it transformed me as well because I knew the spirit of fear that had gripped my life was gone. It's amazing how the Father took me back into a trauma I had experienced as a child, but this time I experienced it through the eyes of faith—faith in a Father I could count on. My stepfather had embodied danger, and his threats were my undoing. This time, though, when I encountered a similar situation, I could cry out to my Abba Father, my Papa. Then God carried me through and brought me out on the other side, fierce and fearless.

Later, I discovered a Bible passage that exactly described what I went through: "Don't worry about anything; instead, pray about everything. Tell God what you need, and thank Him for all He has done. Then you will experience God's peace, which exceeds anything we can understand. His peace will guard your hearts and minds as you live in Christ Jesus" (Philippians 4:6–7).

I literally experienced this verse that day in LA. At first I felt fear, sure I was going to die. But back in that hotel shower, I prayed and I petitioned. (Man, did I petition! Like ugly crying, friend.) And God's peace, which made absolutely no sense, came over me and guarded my heart and my mind. It allowed me to pack up my belongings, drive through a strange city, face gang members telling me how they were going to rape me, and then love on them and come out on the other side stronger.

Yep—this God stuff is no joke! Who's the *She-Ra* beastmaster now? Well, reality check. A big, *bad* angel was probably right behind me with his sword ready to go. Regardless, I knew I was safe. Because if God is for me, who can be against me? No weapon formed against me will prosper. I'm in His hands, and yes, I can do all things through Christ who strengthens me. These assurances from Scripture aren't just empty words; they're real! We don't have to be timid. We don't have to be afraid.

Yet you might think, *Well, that's great for you, Christine, but trying to overcome my fears hasn't worked for me.*

Remember, I was the girl who couldn't walk into her house without flinging open the closet doors and looking behind the living room drapes because of fear. I was a hopeless wreck. But that morning in LA, when fear gripped my heart tight as a wrench, I turned to God. No fancy words. Not even a lot of Bible verses to quote. Just a desperate heart cry. I had nowhere else to go and nothing else to give. And just like God promises, He flooded me with unbelievable peace, the peace that passes all understanding.

God wants to do the same for you. He sees your worries. He sees your anxieties. He understands the fear. He doesn't condemn you for how you feel; He just wants to hold you. He wants to bring you to the other side of fear stronger and bolder, my friend.

We all fear. We all have anxiety. Your life experience might not be as extreme as a creepy rapist guy calling your house, but whatever it is, it's real, and anxiety can take over any life. Maybe you're worried about your kids being bullied at school. Or you're worried about your job after your boss's stinging words following a project you gave your best to but didn't stop the company from losing money. Maybe in the relationship or marriage you're in, you're scared you'll lose him. Or maybe everything's fine, but a voice comes to rob your joy, whispering in your head, "Life can't stay this good. Something is bound to go wrong."

Wherever you are, whatever you're up against, God is for you. *Really.* He's for you! Woman of God, be bold, be fierce! You're strong and courageous, and He promises us this: "God has not given us a spirit of fear, but of power and of love and of a sound mind" (2 Timothy 1:7 NKJV).

Did you catch that? Power. Love. Sound mind. That's pure gold right there. God has big dreams for you. Remember Kintsugi art? God sees the cracks in you, and He can't wait to gently lift your heart broken by fear and press the pieces back together, lining the cracks with His gold. His strong hands can squeeze you back to safety, back to peace. He'll infuse His strength into your areas of fear.

Oh, those cracks will always be there. I still have the memories of Scott's phone calls and of shaking in my living room in my pajamas as a nine-year-old. But the cracks will shine with the gold of power and love where once there was fear. Now I also have the memories of perfect peace as I watched the knife flip in and out of that gang member's hand, of my conversation at the table with those young men as I shared family photos, of the laughter as they walked me to my car, trying to explain that *phat* is bad (which is good). God went to the crack of fear and filled it with His gold. I didn't just get a do-over; I got an upgrade. I'm stronger and braver now than I would have been had those experiences never happened.

You *Can* Overcome Fear

Of course, this story isn't over, because I still had to go to the Staples Center and pick up the Love of my Life. I'm sure I glowed as I recounted the afternoon's drama—how God had given me so much peace and used me to change lives. But . . . Mitch wasn't quite as excited to hear my story as I was to tell it. Now *I* was giddy and *he* was traumatized.

"Babe, that's amazing," he said, "but *never* do that again."

So, here's my disclaimer: Don't go trying to find gang members to overcome your fears. But do go for the crying-out-to-God part, because He hears you. Then trust the journey He has for you, precious one, because if He can give me peace, He will give you peace. He loves everybody, and He offers His peace to everyone, no matter who they are. If fear is gripping you, speak life. Hold your thoughts captive (2 Corinthians 10:5) and speak only what God says about you.

Now let's talk about the difference investing in others makes, just as my hero Jeanne invested in that broken young woman who desperately needed God's gold.

Reflection Questions

⊶ What promise from God's Word can you cling to when you feel afraid?

⊶ How would your life look different if you had God's peace in that area instead of fear?

CHAPTER 2

INVEST IN OTHERS

I tried to ease you into my life's story with the phone call threats in fourth grade, but some of what I still have to share gets even heavier. Praise God, you'll see His redemption in all this. You've got to find the cracks to see the gold.

My mom worked so hard to provide for us. As I said, she sometimes held down three jobs. She often rose at 4:00 a.m., and her work ethic and determination to make it was one of the greatest examples of grit I've ever seen. She never gave up, and her can-do attitude even in the midst of a storm inspired me then and inspires me still.

You've already heard the story about her second husband, Scott, the rapist crazy-guy stepdad who went back to prison after his threatening phone calls to me when I was nine. Mom married again when I was thirteen, bringing dad number three into my life. We'll call him Chuck.

Chuck was more stable than my dad and Scott, and he felt like the father I never had. He took me to school activities, and he signed me up for gymnastics, which I loved. My dreams came true when he officially adopted me, becoming my new forever-dad. Finally, I'd found my place in life.

By this time, my older sister was in her twenties. She was a genius, yet not real high on the whole common sense thing. She would do things like cut my leotards in half so I couldn't wear them to gymnastics. When I started to wear bras, she cut those up too. I know my sister had a lot of problems and pain as well. I think she felt insecure that others had something that she didn't. That's when she would start doing strange stuff. The thing is, she was beautiful, talented, with a crazy-high IQ, and the woman was ten inches taller than I. She had plenty to be happy about. Yet, isn't that what insecurity does? It causes you to believe you're less-than, when really you're exactly the way God wanted you to be.

We lived in a split-level house, and late one night when I was fifteen, I walked down to the kitchen. My sister's bedroom was on the same floor. I must have made a noise, because Chuck flew out of her room. I don't know why he didn't just stay in there, but I heard him say, "Tell her I was in your room because—" But I couldn't catch the rest.

My sister told me whatever lie he'd coached her to tell, and honestly, I probably would have believed her if they hadn't both acted so guilty. I suspected something was up.

The following day is blurry, but I remember standing in the living room telling my mom what happened. She confronted the two of them, and they admitted to having an affair. My dad was cheating on my mom with my sister.

My sister got so angry I told on them, that she started hitting me hard—enough to bruise me. When I fought back, she called the police and accused *me* of attacking *her*. The police came, but they saw right through her story. Still, when they asked me if I wanted to press charges, I said no.

Chuck and my sister left right away, first draining the family bank account, then married as quickly as they could. Now my adoptive father was my brother-in-law, and my sister was my stepmom. It all felt like a bad country music song.

Years later, I found comfort in the fact that this kind of stuff happened in the Bible too (in my big, fat 1 Corinthians family).

Mom collapsed emotionally. She couldn't do life. She went to a psychiatrist and started taking antidepressants, but then she really couldn't function. So I all but ran the household and became *her* mother for a season, just trying to help her get through each day. My sweet mom. I can't imagine how her daughter's betrayal and the simultaneous loss of her husband felt, you know? She went through so much, and I'm sure it was a feat of Herculean strength just to get out of bed.

I wanted to be there for her, but I was lost too. I'd finally had what felt like family, and then poof! It had all been a lie. I didn't know who I was or where I belonged. On top of that, Mom couldn't pay the bills. Creditors took away our television set, then the stereo system, then the car. She filed for bankruptcy, and we had to move into a small apartment. We'd had two poodles, but then one of them died, and we lost the other one because our new place didn't allow pets. Now my life had officially turned into a bad country music song. We even lost the stinkin' dogs!

Of course we couldn't afford for me to continue gymnastics lessons. For a while, the gym let me have them for free in exchange for cleaning. I really thought I was helping them while I flipped from one mirror to the next. But now I realize they just had compassion on a fifteen-year-old whose world had fallen apart.

I couldn't hide my situation from anyone at school either. After I showed up with bruises from the fist fight with my sister, the whole school knew I was in a mess. But no one mentioned it in front of me. No one knew what to say.

I was alone.

Glimmers of Hope

Mom took me to her psychiatrist, who gave me the same antidepressants she was on. But they made me emotionally numb. I woke up, went to school, came home, and then slept, all without feeling much of anything. I was a zombie. After a few days, I quickly reached the level of not caring whether I lived or died. Honestly, dying sounded preferable, so I decided to go for it.

I took a pill bottle from the bathroom medicine cabinet to my room and shut the door. I knew Mom would be the one to find my body, so I wrote her a good-bye letter telling her how much I loved her. Then sitting on the floor, leaning against my bed, pill bottle and letter in front of me, I glanced out my window.

We lived just outside of Salt Lake City at the base of a ski resort. Our neighborhood was sandwiched between mountains, with the resort on one side and Kennecott Copper Mine on the other. The mine was like a giant bowl carved out of rock with mountains surrounding it. It really was a gorgeous place to grow up. Our house was at the top of a hill, and my bedroom window sat just above the peak of our garage. I used to crawl out at night and lie on our roof to watch the stars over the basin, twinkling against the black outlines of the mountains. I could almost feel the mountains surrounding me. I loved those mountains.

Now I decided to go for one last walk as a way of saying good-bye to the world, and that's when I saw this guy from my class out riding a horse.

Chad was a good kid. Me? Not so much. I was the kid who did drugs (and I'm not talking about antidepressants now) and came to school with bruises from fights with my sister. But when I said hi, he dismounted, then talked to me with kindness. I'm sure he'd heard rumors about what had been going on with me, but he didn't bring them up. He just talked to me like we were friends. Like he wanted me to be there. Like I wasn't a burden to him. Like maybe I belonged in the world after all.

Then as I was leaving, Chad said, "See you at school tomorrow."

Back in my room, I slipped the pill bottle into the medicine cabinet, then crumpled the letter and tossed it into my wastebasket.

I was going to school tomorrow.

What Family Can Be

Chad's kindness saved my life that day, giving me a glimmer of hope, and I decided not to give up. Perhaps I had a reason to live after all. (Isn't it interesting that I didn't know God, but I believed there was a God?)

I still had such a long way to go, but I decided that whatever it took, I would make it in life.

I didn't like how the antidepressants numbed me, so I stopped taking them. As soon as I did, every suicidal thought left.[2] But then I remember sitting at my desk in a daze at school, watching the kids around me interacting. As they laughed and shared stories about their weekends, they seemed so . . . normal. How was I supposed to be normal when I didn't even know what normal was?

I suddenly found myself beelining for Sherry, the nicest girl in my class. I was certain she had a normal family, and I asked if I could stay at her house for the week. To my surprise, she said, "Sure. I'll ask my parents."

Again, I was the kid using drugs, not someone you'd want to take home to Mom, let alone stay with your family for a week. I'm not sure Sherry told her parents about the drugs, but she probably told them about the bruises and that I usually ran around with a bad crowd. Still, they must have realized how badly I needed a week away from home because they said yes.

Leaving Mom on her own (I felt desperate for a break), I packed my duffel bag with enough jeans, sweatshirts, and hairspray to last the week (lots of hairspray! It was

---

2   I wish my mom's doctor had told me about possible side effects from and reactions to an antidepressant, such as becoming suicidal. If you're already taking an antidepressant or your doctor wants to prescribe one, be sure to have that conversation. And if you see someone's behavior change after they start taking this kind of medication (or any medication), say something to them. It could save a life.

the eighties, after all) and headed to their house. Sherry had four siblings, and her parents were still married to each other.

That evening, and every evening for the rest of the week, everyone in the family helped make dinner. That in itself was such an anomaly to me. My mom was a trooper, but because she worked so much, I usually made my own meals—consisting mainly of yogurt, cereal, and granola bars. But then Sherry's whole family and I ate dinner together too, which seemed like a miracle. And the kids helped clear the table afterward, which again blew my mind.

The crazy part for me was how Sherry's parents liked each other, even laughing together during dinner. They also talked to their kids about their day. And get this— the family even had an inversion table you could lie on and it would flip you upside down like an antigravity machine. We played with it for a bit, and I loved getting to be a kid again. Then it was time for homework in the living room. Sherry and her siblings sprawled across each other like a litter of puppies. One sibling sat sideways on the couch with her legs stretched over Sherry's lap as they worked. A little brother sat on the floor in front of the couch, leaning against the other sister while he watched TV. They seemed to feel so safe with each other.

I couldn't get enough. That whole week, I was like a fly on the wall, wide-eyed, watching a family love each other. They did their best to love me too, and I wanted to absorb their love, but I wasn't really in a place for that. I soaked it in as much as I could, though. I especially remember Sherry's father being so kind to me.

There was so much love, safety, and warmth there—a glimpse of what true joy looks like.

When I returned home, I told my mom, "You need to get a life." (I was really subtle like that.) She eventually quit taking the antidepressants, but I continued both experimenting with drugs and running with the wrong crowd.

If Sherry's family had kept tabs on my life after that week, they could easily have thought, *What a waste. We took in this girl and loved her for a week, but it made no difference in her life.* But they had no idea how their picture of a kind, loving family—another glimmer of hope—stuck with me. When I had kids of my own and had no idea how to be a good parent, I kept going back to my memories of that week with Sherry's family. They proved to me that loving families did exist.

Filled with Gold

I can relate so much to the story of Joseph in the Bible's book of Genesis. He had a rough life. Because he was his father's favorite son, his brothers hated him.

They even wanted to kill him. One day while they were working in the fields, Joseph's father sent him to check on them. Seizing the opportunity to get rid of him, they sold him to some passing slave merchants. Talk about family dysfunction!

So now he was a slave, taken to Egypt. And on top of that, his master's wife falsely accused him of attempted rape, which put him in prison for years. It would have been so easy for Joseph to give up. I'm sure at moments he felt God had abandoned him and he had nothing left to live for. But here's the thing: bad things happen in life. They just do. It's how you handle them that matters. Joseph made a choice in that prison cell—he could be a victim of someone's cruel act, or he could lead from the place he was in. Joseph chose to lead.

Eventually, Joseph's life turned around. He miraculously interpreted Pharaoh's dream, and Pharaoh released him from prison and promoted him to second-in-command over all of Egypt, next to Pharaoh himself. Then during a famine, Joseph's brothers came to Egypt seeking grain. They didn't recognize him, and Joseph held the power of life or death over them. He chose forgiveness. He told them who he was, welcomed them in friendship, and invited them all to move to Egypt, where they could be cared for.

But after Joseph's father passed away, even after all that kindness, Joseph's brothers were still scared he would take revenge for how they'd treated him. Here's what Joseph told them: "Don't be afraid of me. Am I God, that I can punish you? You intended to harm me, but God intended it all for good. He brought me to this position so I could save the lives of many people" (Genesis 50:19–20).

Looking back on his life, Joseph could see the beauty God had brought from his brokenness. God used Joseph to save an entire nation from famine. He restored Joseph's loss, let him see his father before he passed away, and reunited him with his brothers. It's a beautiful story, and it's one of my favorites.

I feel like Joseph. Looking back, now that I can see the beauty God brought out of the difficulties in my life, I know it was all worth it. Honestly, if I had to do it all over again, I would in a heartbeat. I wouldn't change a thing. The good, the bad, and the ugly—I am who I am because of it.

Was it hard? Oh yes. But because of those moments with Chad and Sherry, I'm a different person. I know the power of receiving kindness from a stranger. We have no idea the power of our words. They could literally save a life. I'm so grateful Chad and Sherry took the time to show me that I mattered.

Precious one, you matter too! Everyone does.

You Can Be Someone's Glimmer

I make friends wherever I go. My kids joke that I talk with more strangers in one week than most people do in twenty years. In fact, as I edit this, my new friend, Ed, whom I just met on the airplane, is helping me with this book. He's looking up Scriptures while we discuss travel plans for our families to meet. He says I need to change "twenty years" to "a lifetime." And it's true, I guess! I've never met a stranger. The way I see it, you never know what's going on in someone else's life. Until you ask. Your kindness might be the one flicker of light—the one glimmer of hope—that encourages them to keep going.

I love to tell people they can change an environment in just thirty seconds. Don't believe me? Try walking into a happy room with a bad attitude and see what happens. But you can also make a difference with a *great* attitude. Leave every person you encounter a little happier when you leave them. Really, it can take only thirty seconds! A smile. A kind word. Try it. I dare you.

I love to ask people questions, like "What are you passionate about?" or "If you had only thirty days to live, what would you do?" or "Why are you sucking air? There must be a great reason."

On a trip to Washington, DC, one of my Uber drivers was the sweetest little old man. (I like to tell people I have an Uber anointing.) He had an accent, so

I asked where he was from, and I learned he had just immigrated to the United States.

"What's the best part about being here?" I asked him, always eager to hear a new story.

He immediately answered, "Opportunities."

"What's the hardest part?"

"Not having friends."

I get that. We chatted a bit about loneliness and friendship. Then I told him, "I'm going to pray and ask God to give you a friend." Then I did pray, out loud, right there in the car.

When I finished, he said, "Okay."

"Okay what?"

"You can write my number down."

"Oh." But I didn't reach for a pen and paper.

Again, just as sweetly, he said, "You can write my number down."

I texted him later that evening. I didn't send a long or fancy message; I just said it was nice to meet him. I wanted him to be encouraged and to know he has value, that he matters. He matters to me. I thanked him for the ride, and then I told him I'd be praying for him. He still texts me every now and then. I guess you could say I keep in touch with my Uber drivers.

Now that man knows someone cares. I mean, can you imagine moving to a new country and not having a single friend? People are starving for kindness! Everyone wants to belong. That desire was built into us, and we yearn for it. So everywhere I go, I like to look for people to encourage, to compliment, and often, to let them know how much God loves them. One day I'll have to write a book about the amazing people I've met just by taking the time to talk to a stranger. Flight attendants, servers, doctors, massage therapists—everyone wants friendship.

Go be the difference you want to see in the world. Be a glimmer of hope. Invest in others.

The Rest of the Story

Years ago, Mitch and I were sitting at a boarding gate in the Seattle airport with our children, waiting for a flight to Hawaii. Our kids had quickly become friends with some other kids there, and I—of course—struck up a conversation with their mom.

At one point, she mentioned her husband was from Utah.

"Oh, no way," I said. "I'm from Utah."

"Really? Where?"

"Sandy."

"That's where my husband's from."

"No way."

"Yeah. He went to Alta High School."

"I went to Alta!"

We discovered her husband was four or five years older than me, so I wouldn't have met him at school. But then she started telling me how fantastic his family was. For instance, every year his parents paid for all the kids and grandkids to go to Hawaii with them.

A thought exploded in my head, and I blurted, "Your husband doesn't have a sister named Sherry, does he?"

"You know Sherry?"

I grabbed her arm, eager to get this done before we all had to board. "I need you to tell your in-laws something for me." I told her how Sherry's family took me in and showed me what a family looks like, a picture that had guided me as a mom ever since.

"Please tell them 'Thank you,'" I said. "They changed my life forever." Then we wept together right there in the airport. I had wished for many years that I had gotten their number. I did, however, find Sherry a couple years ago. I finally had the chance to thank her for her kindness.

Now, it's not uncommon for my hubby to turn around and see people crying as I talk with them. It's his fault, after all! He's prayed over me for the past twenty-some years, knowing I have a Jericho anointing too, meaning I break down walls in people's lives. Now, don't look for that kind of anointing in the Bible; Mitch made it up. Nonetheless, I own it. I walk in it. I love people, and I want them to know they're loved. So if you're in the grocery line with me, you're loved. If you step onto the elliptical next to me, you're loved. If you get stuck on an airplane with me, yep, you're loved!

Yet this time, Mitch saw me in tears as well—tears of joy because I'd had the opportunity to say thank you to someone for changing my life and the lives of many generations to come.

You have no idea the impact you can have on someone. Be present. Look around. Hurting people are all over. When you next go out, find someone to encourage. Invest in others.

Reflection Questions

- ⚬—ℼ Think about a time when you were in difficult circumstances. How did you gain victory in that area of life?
- ⚬—ℼ Looking at your past circumstances, how have you seen God use them for good today?

CHAPTER 3

WALK
IN THE LIGHT

A few years ago, Mitch and I took a trip to Costa Rica, where I connected with someone who runs a nonprofit to help women exploited through sex trafficking. I love what her ministry does in restoring lives.

As we talked outside on a deck, she shared her personal story about coming out of human trafficking, and then she asked about my life. You know how sometimes you meet people and instantly feel like you can tell them anything? She was one of those people for me, and I told her I'd been a dancer at a strip club in my late teens.

She leaned forward in her lawn chair. "Wow. You were trafficked too."

I thought, *What is she talking about?*

"No, I wasn't. I was just a dancer."

"But you were."

"No, I chose to do that." I could see how something else that happened to me in my past qualified as being trafficked because I never chose to do it (I'll tell you about that later in this chapter). But I had, at least on some level, chosen to work as a dancer.

For years, I had been a passionate advocate against human trafficking. I had heard the stories of horrendous abuse—of eight-year-old girls kept in cages in India and raped twenty times a day, of families in Thailand selling their daughters to pimps to gain income. Those girls were victims of sex trafficking. But me? Trafficked as a dancer? No. I would never put myself in the same category as those girls. I wasn't trafficked. Was I?

I thought back on my story . . .

How My Life as a Dancer Began

After that one glorious week at Sherry's house, I went back home to life as I knew it—including using drugs. I also had no idea what a healthy relationship with a man looked like. And no wonder. My experience with men so far had not been great: a biological father who abandoned me, a stepdad who threatened to rape me, and an adoptive father who cheated on my mom with my sister.

At age seventeen, I got pregnant. I chose to keep the baby, one of the best decisions of my life. My first daughter, Melissa, was born one week after I turned eighteen.

I dropped out of high school and moved from Utah to California, where I got a job as a telemarketer at a meatpacking company. They told me I was selling meat, but I soon realized we sold the meat in deep freezers, and to get the meat, our customers had to buy a freezer too. I was supposed to trick them into buying a freezer by first selling them meat. Over the phone. Through cold calls. (Freezing cold calls.) *That* was a fun job—not! To make things worse, I got paid by commission, and let's just say sales were arctic.

I felt the pressure of not making enough money. How could I ever provide for my baby this way?

As I was driving home from work one morning, I passed a strip club and wondered if I could earn enough there to survive. Soon—and with fear and trembling—I walked through the club's doors and was instantly hit with the smell of cigarette smoke and the sound of rap music blaring from the speakers. The building had no windows, so it was dark inside, with only colored lights shining on the stage. A girl in skimpy lingerie danced on a stage raised only a foot above the floor, and men were scattered around tables, sitting with other barely clothed women.

I couldn't handle it. I left. I couldn't get out fast enough.

Time went by, and as the pressure to earn more income mounted, I would walk into the club only to leave but then return again.

One time, one of the men approached me. "Are you looking for a job?"

"I am."

He looked me up and down. "Come on back."

We passed the lounge area, where women were performing lap dances and other favors on couches. Some were topless. My stomach clenched.

The guy took me to the dressing room, where it was much quieter as the girls changed clothes or waited to get on stage. He explained the logistics of working as a dancer. I would pay him a certain amount, then I could keep the rest, plus any tips I made. I could make over a thousand dollars in a single night, he said. And here I was squeaking out $4.25 an hour plus commission! (But never mind the commission—that never happened.) Dancing at the club seemed like a no-brainer.

I went back to the club floor and sat and watched the girl on stage dance around the pole.

There's no way.

I couldn't do it.

I walked out.

I went back to my telemarketing job that evening, but I felt stuck between two nightmares. I hated the club, but I also hated my current job. Sometimes I made no money at all, and the guy I was with at the time couldn't handle that. I paid the price. He would disappear for days at a time, with no warning and no word of his location. I felt worthless, and I was terrified he'd keep leaving. I felt like I had to please him no matter the cost. Making a thousand dollars a night started sounding really great.

So I worked up the courage to go back to the club, and I sat and talked to the girls, trying to get used to the idea of working there. But I just couldn't. They were sweet and encouraging, but I could tell they didn't like what they were doing.

Finally, after more long nights as a telemarketer, I went back to the club. One of the girls suggested I start with her dance outfit, but as we stood in the dressing room, I couldn't do it.

I told the manager, "I'm so sorry. I just can't."

The next thing I knew, he was out on the floor announcing, "We have a new girl, and she's scared. Can everyone help her out?" Men began to cheer, and I felt like there was no backing out.

Before I left the dressing room, the girl whose outfit I wore gave me a pep talk for how to mentally handle this job. "Do you see those hooks?" she said as she gestured toward one of the walls. Hooks lined about two feet of it, like places to hang coats in a school classroom.

"Here's what you have to do," she continued. "Before you go on stage, take your Christine self and hang her on a hook. Then while you're out there, become the girl who dances. When you're done for the night, come back in here, put on your Christine self. Then when you leave the club's doors, you're Christine again. This is the only way you can survive."

I swallowed, nodded, and walked out to the club floor with her. But I still couldn't bring myself to start. Then someone took me by the hand, walked me onto the stage, and there I was.

That's how I began my career as a dancer.

Dark and Light

It was a horrible experience, and I felt like I was going to throw up. But it was kind of like jumping off a sheer cliff. Once I took the leap, I had no way to climb back up. And the job didn't get easier after that. The money was good, but I always felt so sick. I survived only by hanging up my Christine self, like the other dancer taught me. That's how we all did it. We all learned to put on an act, especially for tips. But every single girl I knew didn't just dislike what they were doing; they hated it as much as I did. We just disconnected who we were outside the club from who we were inside the club. Or at least we tricked ourselves into thinking we could.

No crack of sunlight ever entered the building. Business hours began at 5:00 p.m., but even in the summer with hours of daylight to enjoy, we entered into darkness. None of us could have tolerated the light exposing our reality anyway. And the real darkness was just the beginning.

Everything about the club was designed to crush human connection and deny all feelings. The customers were using us to numb their pain. And the girls who worked there? Many of us were high on drugs and alcohol. It was hard to work that job sober. The music was so loud you couldn't talk to anyone unless you both yelled. But let's be honest, no one was there to talk. We were *all* trying to numb ourselves.

Part of me hates sharing these stories with you. But Jesus has been so merciful. So merciful. And the only way to show His deep mercy is to tell you where I came from.

Paul writes in Ephesians, "Take no part in the worthless deeds of evil and darkness; instead, expose them. It is shameful even to talk about the things that ungodly people do in secret. But their evil intentions will be exposed when the light shines on them, for the light makes everything visible" (Ephesians 5:11–14).

We dancers were in literal darkness, and so were the men we serviced. Everyone was desperately trying not to be exposed. Like the above passage states, it's shameful even to talk about what we did behind closed doors. When Satan controls your life, he doesn't settle for halfway destroying it; he pushes you as deep into the darkness as he can. But even while working at the club, I still knew God was real. I remember telling both customers and dancers, "You need Jesus!" Even before I knew Him, my life was marked by God. And in His mercy, He was about to illuminate my darkness.

That's my goal with this book—to throw back the curtains and let the sunlight flood in, so you can see how far God has brought me. The cracks run deep, but His gold shines all the more brilliantly because of the depth of darkness I lived in. I promise you, wherever you are in life, whatever you've gone through, He can do the same for you. He is the Light of the world. When darkness is exposed, it gives way to the light.

Beloved one, walk into the light and name your brokenness. But don't let your shame hinder you from being the radiant woman of God you were created to be. Let him mend you with His gold.

Sinking

I hated working at the club, but I didn't think I had a way out. Then about a year after I'd started working there, I discovered I was pregnant again. This time

I was having twins, Tyler and Dylan (the most beautiful identical boys you could lay your eyes on). I was pressured to work almost to the end of my pregnancy. Talk about a sad picture. The nine-month-pregnant stripper on the stage because she needs the money.

The first twin was born naturally and the second through emergency C-section. I lost so much blood that I had to stay in the hospital for a week. After coming home, I rested for six weeks and then started dancing again. But my body hadn't fully recovered. While performing one night, I started bleeding and had to be rushed to the hospital. It was awful. I desperately wanted to stop dancing, but that was simply not an option. At one point, I even got a job at Circuit City. I was so excited, but the guy I was with insisted that wasn't a real job. He threatened to leave me unless I continued working at the club.

I was nineteen years old when the twins were born, and now I had three kids—a toddler and two infants. I was also working until two or three in the morning and crashed as soon as I got home. My kids, however, woke up a few hours later, ready to start the day. They had needs, and I was exhausted.

One day I was talking to a friend about how hard my life was. She said, "Oh, honey, you need speed." That's methamphetamine, or "meth" for short.

"Why?" I asked. "What does it do to you?"

"When you take it, you don't have to sleep. You have all the energy in the world."

Oh my goodness, I thought. *That's exactly what I need.* (Real bright, I know.) So I started taking speed, which began my road to drug addiction. I didn't take the drugs because I didn't love my kids but because I did. I wanted to be awake to care for them during the day, and soon I was taking in speed like morning coffee. I didn't touch it any other time of day, but I quickly grew dependent on it. I couldn't function unless I took it each morning.

Now I was dancing *and* truly addicted to drugs. I still wanted to quit dancing, but I also still didn't think I had a choice. I needed the income. The longer I stayed in that lifestyle, though, the more I hated life. I hated people. I stole from them and lied to them. I cussed like a sailor. I was bitter, angry, and unforgiving.

Sinking Lower

I didn't think I could sink any lower, but I did. And this is what I thought my friend in Costa Rica was referring to when she said I had been trafficked.

The friend who recommended I take speed wanted to go to a club one night, and I agreed to go with her. Once there, she offered me some meth. It looked different, though. It was brown and more granular. She said, "Oh, it's just a really pure form." And for some reason I can't explain, I took it. At night.

The next thing I knew, I was waking up in a strange house, lying on my back with a large man raping me. I was aware of everything, but I couldn't seem to move. I remember his sweat dripping on my face and how it felt trying to escape. It was like a dream where you know you need to run, but your legs won't work.

Then I saw my friend watching us, and I wondered why she wasn't helping me. Then all I could do was cry. I'd been betrayed. And I couldn't move because of the drugs.

Afterward, I found my clothes, put them on, and got into this girl's car, where she handed me money. My first thought was, *If I take this money, I'll be a prostitute.* But I also didn't want her to have it after she'd used me.

I took it.

Trafficked

Sitting on that deck in Costa Rica, I paused to reflect. I could see how being drugged and raped qualified as sex trafficking, but what about my dancing at the club? I wasn't so sure that fit the bill. Hadn't I just made a bad choice? I never once saw myself as a victim as a dancer. But my friend wouldn't give up the topic.

"Why do you think you're so passionate about helping women who have been trafficked?" she asked again.

"Because it's wrong," I told her.

"But think about your time as a dancer. Did someone profit financially from your body?"

"Yes."

"Did you want to quit?"

"Oh, absolutely. Every single day."

"Were you forced to do it?"

"Yes. I was even dancing again six weeks after I had the twins. I didn't have a choice. I had to make money."

"Were you threatened when you tried to quit?"

"Yes."

"Now tell me, Christine, what exactly is the definition of trafficking?"

It finally clicked. Yes, I had been trafficked. Me. But up till that moment, I'd never seen it that way because trafficking in America looks very different from what we think it does. When you think about strippers or prostitutes, remember these are broken women, most often forced into this work with few if any other options for survival. They're also, like so many young people, starving to be loved.

Parents teach their kids about stranger danger, telling them not to climb into a creepy guy's van. That's great. Yet for the most part, stranger danger looks more like this: "Hey, you're pretty." A trafficker knows by that statement whether they can traffic someone or not. They know when they've found someone vulnerable to a person who makes them feel wanted or secure or just able to survive. Then they're trapped, forced to do things they never wanted to do.

Let's ensure our daughters and sons know they're valuable, making them secure in our love so they'll recognize a phony who's peddling counterfeit love, and turn and run.

If you're forced to do something with your body for someone's financial gain, dear one, that is trafficking. My mind was blown when I realized this. If this is a situation you or a loved one is in, please reach out to the National Human Trafficking Hotline at 888-373-7888.

My Coming to Jesus Moment

After the rape, I was devastated. In my job as a dancer, I had to pretend I liked men, but I wanted to claw out their eyes and spit in their faces. Worse, I could still justify my work as a dancer, but I'd always seen prostitutes as epic failures, and now I'd all but become one by taking that money. That realization crushed me.

I decided men were horrible, and I never wanted anything to do with them again. That's when I began living a gay lifestyle.

After my first relationship, which didn't last very long, I started spending more time with my best friend, who was gay. We would go to clubs or hang out at gay bars. Or the kids and I would go to her house and hang out there. I thought, *this is it. I'm totally gay. This is why I have all these problems with men.*

But I wasn't happy, and my three precious kids were my only source of joy, the only thing that kept me going. I wanted so much to be a good mom, yet I was addicted to drugs.

One morning I woke up to one of my babies crying. It was the hurt cry every mama knows. As I was running down the stairs, I thought, *Oh, I should do some drugs first*, and then it hit me. I had just chosen drugs over my child. How had I come to this?

I was so broken. Everything in my life was spiraling out of control, and I finally realized just how low I'd sunk. If there was a God, I needed Him—desperately. I needed a Savior, because I sure wasn't able to save me from myself. And I knew that's what Jesus was supposed to be. I can't even recall when or how I first heard about Him, yet I'd been telling the other dancers they needed Him. Now that I'd hit rock bottom, I realized how badly I needed Him myself.

I fell to my knees and cried, "Jesus, if You're real, my life is Yours. If You can do anything for me, I give it all to You." One by one, I listed my sins—the drugs, the alcohol, the men and the women, the dancing, the stealing. Everything. I named my brokenness. And I meant it when I said He could have it all. If He could help me, I'd never go back to any of it.

Then I so tangibly felt the presence of God. Immediately, I went and threw away all my drugs. From then on, I never turned back. Every single one of those promises I made to God that morning, I kept. I have never gone back.

Right then, I caught a glimpse of what I had felt in Sherry's home back in high school. I felt love. I'm sure that family thought, *What a waste of time having this girl in our home when she just turned around and did all those bad things anyway.* But now the moment had come that changed my life and the course of my family's life forever. I didn't know how to get to where Sherry's family was, but I knew I was going to.

When I came to Christ, I was able to immediately give up every negative aspect of my old life. I know that's not the case for most, but I supernaturally had the ability to completely walk away. I threw away my drugs, but I never had one day of withdrawal. I never had one temptation or desire to go back. Alcohol was gone. The gay lifestyle was gone, every ounce of that desire disappearing completely, never to return. I just turned from all those ways and never looked back. I was a new creation in Christ.

I also started going to church, seeking the Lord, reading my Bible. It's like God had said, *Yep, you're terrible at this. How about you let Me help you now? How about you try this life over here, honey?*

Now I'm so passionate about telling others about the love of Jesus. And if He could do that for a wretch like me—someone who felt she had no value, no worth—what could He do for you? Everything. If you name your brokenness and give it all to Him, He can fill the cracks with His gold.

Oh, and my little guy who was crying?

He was fine too.

Reflection Questions

○── What areas in your life do you feel that, if they were exposed, there's no way God could love you, nor could anyone else?

○── How could you allow the light to shine in that area so you can be set free?

CHAPTER 4

TRUST GOD FOR HIS PROVISION

After I gave my heart to Jesus, I moved back to Utah, where I found a recovery group that gave me stability and helped me cope with life. They also had family programs and kids' activities, which was great. I loved the connection and encouragement, only it lacked Jesus.

The kids and I bounced from friend to friend, sleeping on couches or wherever we could stay. Then we stayed in my mom's basement, even though it was the tiniest thing—just the size of a bedroom with one small bed. Each night the four of us slept crammed together, and between the kids' kicking and squirming, I couldn't sleep.

Then a guy at my recovery group offered us a twin bed. That might seem like a small thing, but it was a massive blessing for me. I could finally get a full night's sleep.

That period was the toughest season of my life, yet it was also the most beautiful. For the first time, I felt free and safe, and my children were safe.

I passionately sought the Lord in every way.

Giving Out of Lack

After giving my life to God, right away I felt freedom. I felt hope. I was incredibly determined to show my children what I had felt that week at Sherry's. I immediately started going to church and seeking the Lord.

So back in California, I had packed up my kids and taken them to church every week. There I was in church, a single mom dressed in a miniskirt and low-cut top, with three small children. You could say I didn't quite fit in. But hey, I tried to be consistent. After we moved to Utah, I visited a church in that same denomination. But so much of the teaching there was about how to please your spouse, which wasn't relevant to my life at that point. I decided to tell the leader how I felt.

"I don't feel like I fit in," I told him.

"You need to attend our singles church," he said.

"Okay, great. Do they have a pretty good children's program?"

"Single people don't have children."

I was floored. "This one does."

"Well, then, once you remarry, you can come back to this church."

"Are you saying my children aren't allowed to go to church here?"

"Oh no, no, no, I'm not saying that. Just not until you get married again."

I stopped going to church then and began simply seeking the Lord for myself. It was a beautiful season of prayer and just getting to know Him. But during that time, I didn't have a job. To work, I needed childcare, but childcare cost more than the income I would earn at any job I was qualified for.

Finally, I had only forty dollars left. I didn't know government assistance existed, and my mom didn't have any money to loan me. So I sat on my bed in her basement, fanned out all my bills, and stared at them.

I can't even put a dent in any of these, I thought. *There's no way. I don't know how I'm going to do this.* But then I thought, *I don't think God will punish me if I just give it all to Him. He's already rescued me from so much. Maybe He can help me here.*

The only person I knew who attended church was the guy who gave me the bed. I wrote a check for that forty dollars, then handed it to him as soon as I could.

"Can you give this money to your church?" I asked.

He agreed, having no idea that check was literally the last penny I had and that I had no way to provide for my babies. I just trusted God.

From that point on, God provided. People helped me buy food. Unexpected gifts came in. God's promise proved true. The birds don't worry about where they are going to rest, and if God also counted every hair on my head, I knew that whether my kids had food mattered to Him.

Dating Mitch

One of the first times I met My Mitch, we were at a recovery meeting. It was a grief counseling group for anybody who had hurts and wounds. I was still working through my issues, and in his grief over losing his first marriage, Mitch had joined this group as well. Eventually, he became one of the leaders there.

One day, members of the group and their families had dinner together at a restaurant. Melissa was four and Tyler and Dylan were two—and, thankfully, potty trained. The twins needed to go to the bathroom before we left, and I was about to take them to the ladies' room when they said, "We don't want to go in the *girls'* bathroom!"

"Okay, you guys go ahead. I'm right here, and I can see the door."

They took forever, and when I started getting worried, I looked around for any man I could send in to check on them.

Then I saw Mitch was still there. I didn't really know him, but I asked if he could check on my boys.

"Oh, sure, no problem," he said before ducking inside the men's room. But then he took forever, too, and I really got worried.

Finally Mitch came out all wide-eyed.

"Was everything okay in there?" I asked.

"Well, you know, they had to go poop, so they wanted me to wipe them."

I groaned.

"And when I walked in, their shoes were on one side of the room, their pants were on the other side, their underwear and shirts somewhere else. So then I gathered their clothes and tried to put them on, but they were like, 'No, that's my brother's shirt.' So you might need to help me sort their clothes. I still couldn't find one sock. Sorry."

I just stood there shaking my head. "Thank you."

And that's how Mitch met Tyler and Dylan. That's commitment, huh?

At this point, I still despised men passionately, but through the recovery group, Mitch and I became better and better friends. Then after months of friendship, we each went on a camping trip with friends.

Mitch had a boat, and while some of us were out on it, one of the girls started telling him about a single friend she wanted to set him up with. She went on and on about how great this girl was, and I realized my heart had dropped. *But I like him! Me!* So there I was, freaking out but trying to act like nothing was going on with me. I'd had no idea I liked Mitch until that moment.

Mitch kept telling her no, though. "I have my eye on someone else," he said.

Then sadness hit. I thought, *If he's turning down that great girl, he must really like this other girl.* That night as I lay in my tent, all I could think about was how sad I was and how much I didn't want him to date anyone else.

The next day, Mitch asked me to go for a walk, and then he asked if I would date him.

"I thought you had your eye on someone else."

"Christine," he said, laughing, "I was looking at you when I said that! 'I've got my *eyes* on someone else.'"

For our very first date, Mitch wanted to take the kids along, so from the first moment, I realized he fully understood what he was getting into. And the first time he had me over to his house, all the kids came as well. Afterward, he called and said, "Um, have you seen any of my doorstops?"

"Your doorstops?"

"Yeah. Every doorstop in my house is missing."

After we were married and the kids and I had moved into his house, one of the kids melted a crayon over a heat vent. I pulled out the vent to clean it and found every single one of those doorstops shoved down inside the heater vent. At least he knew what he was getting into.

When Mitch proposed, we had both been married before, and we wanted to do something fun and different for this wedding. So we decided on a Renaissance theme. But back in the nineties, you couldn't find unique wedding dresses ready-made. So I thought, *Hey, I'm a great seamstress. I'll just make my dress.* (Did I mention I had only two months to do it?) I bought the pattern I liked, and I was super excited to get going.

Well, I laid out the pattern on my living room floor, and then I started to cry. I didn't know how to sew! I had made draperies, and they were so stinking awesome that I really thought I was a great seamstress. But I had never seen a pattern before in my life. The drapes had been just big squares of fabric.

Mitch said, "How about I make your wedding dress?" (Mitch had never seen a pattern either.)

So my *fiancé* made my wedding dress, and it was gorgeous.

Learning to Trust

I married Mitch when I was twenty-four. Our daughter Ariel was born when I was twenty-five. She was my fourth child and Mitch's first.

But only three months into the pregnancy, I was already dilated to a two and 90 percent effaced, which meant I could give birth at any moment. For the next six months, then, I had to take medication to prevent labor and lie flat on my back. I could not be upright, period. I even had to eat lying down. It was a scary time for us.

This forced Mitch to become not only a new father to my oldest three children but also mom, doctor, chef, and housekeeper. It forced me to trust him with my children—now *our* children. This was a good thing, because right after the wedding, I was the mama bear, ready to take out anyone! After all, I had been so hurt by men in the past, and my first instinct was to protect my kids at all costs.

So when Mitch tried to parent the kids, I interfered. I wanted him to be their father and be close to them, but not that close. And my behavior hindered the growth of our family. But in His graciousness, God allowed me to get pregnant right away—and not just any pregnancy but one requiring full bed rest, so I was forced to trust Mitch to be my children's father.

You name it, he did it, and he did it with joy. It blessed our family for Mitch to essentially become the sole parent for those six months, and it was the best thing that could have happened to me then. I had no choice but to release my children to Mitch and trust he could take care of them.

Those months of bed rest grew our relationship and taught me that I could trust a man and be safe. And not just a man but a God who provides.

God Gives Me Gwen

Right before I was put on bed rest, we threw a birthday party for Tyler and Dylan. They were in preschool, so we invited the kids from their class. The boys really liked one little guy named Gus. I had never met him or his mom before, but her name was Gwen. She was tall and thin with tan skin, dark hair, and deep, dark eyes. She was absolutely beautiful. We talked for only about five minutes before she left.

Then when I was put on bed rest, Gwen just showed up at our home.

"I heard," she said. "What can I do for you?"

I didn't know her, so I just said, "Maybe you could just pray for us."

We weren't smart enough back then to have meal trains or any sort of coordinated care. Thankfully, Gwen wasn't satisfied with my answer.

"But I understand your husband and mom both work all week during the day. Here's what I can do. Your daughter's in kindergarten, right?"

"Yeah."

"Gus and I will come here every day and get her ready and off to school. Then I'll get your boys ready for preschool and take them there with Gus. Later, I'll pick them up, and then your guys can hang out at my house until your mom gets off work to help you. You said she gets off at 2:30?"

"Yeah."

"Then I'll just bring them back at 2:30. I can do this as long as you need me to."

I'm thinking, *Who are you?* I had met this lady for only five minutes at a birthday party, and she was offering to take care of my kids every weekday for the next six months? Crazy! But I had no other plan in place, and I needed the help.

Gwen showed up every day, and not only did she get the kids ready for school, but she cooked, folded laundry, and cleaned. She was a godsend. She was perfect, absolutely perfect. She baked for me and brought me anything I needed. She even brought me magazines. She also sat and talked with me during those long days of bed rest. She never gossiped, never got annoyed with the kids. She was a dream come true. I don't know what I would have done without her.

Six months later, I gave birth to Ariel. Gwen visited me at the hospital, and she was holding little Ariel in her arms when she said, "I have some news for you. We're moving."

I was heartbroken. "To where?"

"Out of town." That was all the information she would give me.

After that day, Gwen stopped answering her phone, and as soon as I was released from the hospital, we drove to her house. It was empty. They had already moved out. We had been seeing each other every day for the past six months, and never once had she mentioned moving. But she'd become my best friend. She helped me through everything. And then the day Ariel was born, she left, never to be seen again.

Someone said to me, "She was an angel." Then I looked up the meaning of the name Gwen. It means "white, pure, blessed, holy." I don't know if Gwen was an angel, but you never know when you're entertaining one or one is entertaining you.

Don't Worry. Trust.

In Luke 5, Simon—also known as Simon Peter or Peter—is washing his fishing nets with his brothers when a crowd pushes Jesus closer and closer to the shore. Jesus steps into Simon's boat and asks him to push it into the water so He can teach the Word of God from there. When He's finished, He tells Simon, "Go out where it is deeper, and let down your nets to catch some fish" (verse 4).

Simon tells him, "Master . . . we worked hard all last night and didn't catch a thing. But if you say so, I'll let the nets down again" (verse 5).

Simon is probably thinking, *What's the point?* But he agrees. And then he's met with net-breaking, boat-sinking success. Luke tells us, "This time their nets were so full of fish they began to tear!" (verse 6).

Simon had strived all night with no results. Then Jesus came into the picture, and Simon and his brothers instantly had so many fish that other people had to come help them. We never need to wonder if God will provide. He did for Simon. He did for me. And He will for you.

We're told Simon was awestruck, and "he fell to his knees before Jesus and said, 'Oh, Lord, please leave me—I'm such a sinful man'" (verse 8). How many of us have had the same fears Simon must have had? But what does Jesus tell him in verse 10? "Don't be afraid!"

Don't be afraid? Seriously? Not "Why did you doubt Me?" or "Hey, I told you so!" Instead, "Don't be afraid!"

Now, why would Jesus say that?

Maybe He knew Simon had been afraid he wouldn't have enough that day. Maybe He knew, when He asked Simon to become one of His first disciples, that deep inside, Simon would be afraid his leader might not always meet his needs.

He might step into your life and say, "Why don't you try this way?"

When I had nothing, God spoke to me through this story about a fisherman, saying, *I am your provider*. I knew I could trust Him, and with that check for forty dollars, He found me faithful down to my last penny. And then He gave me a job.

If we seek first His kingdom and His righteousness, the Lord will give us everything we need (Matthew 6:33). We just need faith for that.

Jesus followed up by making an announcement to Simon Peter and his brothers: "From now on you'll be fishing for people!" (verse 10). Then, putting his faith in Jesus, Simon laid down his nets and followed Him (Mark 1:17–18).

Oh, I should mention this: the man I gave that check to is the love of my life, Mitch Soule!

Reflection Questions

- In what areas do you need God's provision for in your life right now? What would it look like for God to meet this need?
- We gain faith by remembering what God has done in our lives. When have you seen God's provision in the past? Rehearse the miracles in your mind.

CHAPTER 5

GIVE OF YOUR RESOURCES

Soon after we were married, Mitch's software business moved to Washington State, and after Ariel was born, we moved there too.

We moved into a very small, old home. Mitch drove the scariest old, red truck. It jolted us around like we were on the Mad Tea Party teacup ride at Disneyland, and I was always afraid to get into it. My neck hurt every time we drove somewhere.

We could afford a bigger home and new truck, but we were attending a tiny Lutheran church that taught wealth was sinful. Like, just plain wrong. If you were rich, you were a sinner. So the more money Mitch made, the guiltier we felt. We tried just giving much of it to the church, but we didn't want anybody to know how much we made. Also, the more we gave, the more money flowed in. It's really true—you can't out-give God.

We thought maybe we could just move to Africa and build an orphanage. Foolproof, right?

Then after our twins were miraculously healed (more on that later), we decided to attend another church that didn't teach wealth was sinful. But we still continued to live with the same guilt. Then our new church hosted a conference called Prosperity with a Purpose. At the conference, Nathanael Wolf, who authored the book *The Gatekeepers*, spoke about the gifts God infuses into His church. He read 1 Corinthians 12:28, which lists people gifted, for instance, to be apostles, prophets, and teachers. Others are helpers—given the gift of "helps."

"What do you guys think 'helps' is?" He asked. "Most people think that it's the janitor or the nursery volunteer. But working in a nursery is not a gift. That's a mandate. Just do it. Being a janitor is not a gift. You're not anointed to be a janitor; that's something everyone should do. Just go pick up the trash. So what is 'helps'? Helps is what funds the most expensive word in the Bible: 'Go.' In order for pastors, prophets, and evangelists to be able to do what they do, they need funding."

Nathanael's teaching was revolutionary for Mitch and me.

In church culture, we tend to do a pendulum swing in our view of money. Either money is bad, leading to what Mitch and I experienced in the church we attended, or it's so good that it leads to believing prosperity is everything, even leading to greed and selfishness. Either view is unhealthy, but in this area, I believe God wants perfect balance.[3]

The Bible talks about provision, prosperity, blessing, and wealth. God desires for us to prosper, but what are we doing with our financial prosperity? What is our heart's motive? Do we desire to fund the kingdom of God, or do we just want more stuff? Are our actions God-based or selfish? And are we willing to surrender our resources when called to do so, whether they are many or few?

Through the conference, Mitch and I realized we are helpers gifted to create wealth, and that gifting is an essential part of ministry. Our mind-set was completely changed. Before, we thought we had to personally do missionary work to be righteous and loved by God. But then we understood that funding ministry is a critical role in the body of Christ. Money serves a great purpose. Without it, it's harder for the kingdom of God to grow. God has work to do, and He does His work through His people. If people aren't willing and obedient to give of their resources, their treasures, then the kingdom won't be preached to the ends of the earth.

It's all God's, 100 percent His.

---

3   In other words, God wants to provide for us and see us prosper, but he doesn't want us to be materialistic, motivated by personal gain rather than generosity and the spreading of his kingdom. Compare, for example, Genesis 13:2–6, Deuteronomy 8:18, and Proverbs 11:25 with Matthew 6:24 and Hebrews 13:5.

As Mitch's business began to grow exponentially, we no longer felt guilty about our income. And you should never feel guilty for desiring a raise, a promotion, or a better job; just check your spirit as to why you want them. People misquote 1 Timothy 6:10 all the time. They say, "Money is the root of all evil." Not accurate! That verse actually says, "The *love* of money is the root of all evil" (KJV, emphasis mine). Big difference!

And Then God Gave Me . . . Inventions!

Over the years, as Mitch and I have learned more about our God-given calling to help fund the kingdom of God, we've also become passionate about generosity. One of the projects we've been especially passionate about is the Museum of the Bible in Washington, DC. God spoke to us about what to give and how to structure our gifts, but after that was all set up, I had the lingering feeling it wasn't enough. We needed to give more. But to do that, we needed to make more.

When I was praying about it, the Lord said, "*Well, do what you know.*" So I thought about what I knew. Cake artistry. I decorate cakes. And instantly, ten different inventions for cake decorating came to mind.

Wow, I thought. I wrote them all down, and then I called our friend Steve Green, president of Hobby Lobby and cofounder of the Museum of the Bible. I shared my ideas and told him if he was interested in these ideas, I wanted proceeds from any sales to go to the Museum of the Bible.

"Those ideas are amazing," he said. "You got them all at once?"

"Yeah."

"Let me put you in touch with the Hobby Lobby baking department."

He transferred me, and after I told the woman my ideas, she said, "Uh, yeah, that's God. But I think you need to get some patents first."

Mitch and I researched patent attorneys, then planned to go with some ones we found in the Seattle area. But we hadn't visited them yet when I had my prayer group over one day. The woman who leads the group walked in and said, "Christine Soule, God spoke to me about you today. He is so proud of you for wanting to give proceeds from your cake decorating ideas to the Museum of the Bible. He wanted to let you know that was a test. He's going to give you more inventions, just kissing you on the cheek and saying, 'Here's some for you.'"

"Oh, well, fantastic," I said, then thought nothing more of it.

Later, a friend of ours told Mitch, "I think you're supposed to talk to a friend of mine who is a patent attorney." Mitch told him we'd already decided to go through someone else, but when he told me about the conversation, he said he thought we should talk to the man.

I trusted Mitch's judgment. We called that patent attorney, and as he started describing his work, I realized he was a for-real genius. He'd worked on the patents for the color-changing LED lightbulb and other billion-dollar technologies. *He's epic*, I thought. *He's off-the-charts amazing.* And here I was thinking, *Well, you know. I've got this really cool spatula.*

I loved talking with him, but I knew he wasn't the right one for my cake ideas. They had nothing to do with technology.

The next morning, I woke up with a complete technology invention in my head. Now, I'm the least technological person on the planet. My husband owns a software company, and I leave all that to him. I decorate cakes and make babies.

But God gave me the idea for this invention. I didn't know if it was any good, but I told Mitch about it.

"Wow," he said. "You need to write that down."

I felt awed. God had set us up with a technology patent attorney before I even knew He'd give me this invention—an answer before I even had a question. If the invention had come to me a day earlier, I probably would have dismissed it, not having any idea what to do about it. But because of the call the day before, I knew exactly where to go.

I called the genius attorney, and he put together a patent portfolio, which actually included twenty-eight separate patents. Then he said, "This could be a billion-dollar idea." And believing profits are in God's hands, we were led to designate the majority of profits split between the museum, Providence Heights, and our partners in the invention.

Isn't it interesting that God told me, *Do what you know*, before leading me to this invention? Sometimes He leads us one step at a time because we can't handle the big picture. It doesn't mean you didn't hear Him when something didn't happen like you thought. Sometimes that's what it takes to prepare you for what He is really wanting you to do. A quote from Andy Stanley's book, *Visioneering*, says, "Be stubborn about the vision. Be flexible with your plan."[4]

Allow God to move and weave in your life as if it were a beautiful dance. Be willing to surrender your resources for the edification of His kingdom, and He will.

---

4 Andy Stanley, *Visioneering: Your Guide for Discovering and Maintaining Personal Vision* (Sisters, OR: Multnomah Books, 2012) , 158.

Walk by Faith, Not by Sight

Giving is really about listening and doing what God says to do with our resources. It's about trusting Him and obeying Him.

My cousin Marcee—who lives in Oregon, functions at about a third-grade level, and uses a walker—wanted to visit us over a weekend. Her brother sent her to us by train because that mode of transportation is easiest for her.

I kept meaning to cancel an appointment at a facial clinic in a nearby town's mall, yet I had never managed to do it. I needed to, though, because it would be difficult for Marcee to walk through the mall.

Then as I was about to make the call, God told me, *You are not canceling the appointment. You need to speak to your esthetician.*

"Okay," I said.

And take him a gift.

"What gift?"

A baby blanket.

I keep a stash of baby blankets with Scripture verses or Christian sayings on them to give to new moms, a resource God obviously knew I had. However, I had some concerns.

"Um, Lord? The man is gay. I don't think he has a baby. Also, I don't know what to do with my cousin if I go. I'm concerned about her being able to walk that far."

The appointment was so close to when Marcee's train for home was leaving that I wouldn't have time to leave her at our house, go to the mall, then pick her up and take her to the train station on time. But since God was telling me to do this, I believed taking her with me would work out somehow. I trusted Him enough to obey Him.

I chose a baby blanket with the beginning of Psalm 46:10 on it: "Be still, and know that I am God." Then I grabbed a note card and wrote this guy, letting him know God told me to give him the blanket so he could wrap himself in God's love, that God wanted him to know the Father's love. Then I sealed the envelope and wrapped the gift.

As we drove to the appointment, I prayed, *Lord, I still don't know what to do about Marcee.*

This mall had a Starbucks, and I thought maybe I could get her situated there with some food and she'd stay put during my appointment. I really didn't want to leave her all by herself, though.

As soon as I opened the door to the coffee shop, I saw one of my friends sitting inside.

"What are you doing here?" I asked her.

"It's the weirdest thing. My car just quit working."

"Oh. So strange," I said, but I knew God was in it. "Since you're here, though, would you mind sitting with my cousin for a little bit while I go to an appointment here in the mall?"

"I'd be happy to," she said.

I bought Marcee something to eat, sat her down with my friend, and left.

When I sat down in the chair at the clinic, my esthetician and I launched into the usual chit-chat. But then I said, "So this is kind of strange, but I brought you a gift."

"You brought me a gift?"

"Yeah," I said, smiling, "and I have a card too." I handed him both, and he opened the envelope, then slid out the card and read it.

He started to cry.

"My mom died, and I just found out who my father is with a DNA testing kit. He was in the company's DNA database. He's Jewish, and he lives in Israel."

God knew what I didn't. This man had never known his father's love, and God wanted him to know his heavenly Father.

Walking in obedience never requires us to figure things out before we take a step. I just needed to trust God. I would never have known what my esthetician was experiencing if I hadn't.

There was also no way I could have known my friend would be in Starbucks to care for Marcee during my appointment. Abraham walked up the mountain to sacrifice his only son in blind obedience, not knowing why God was asking this of him or how it would work out. And then right when he was about to kill his son, God provided a lamb caught in the thicket. Abraham sacrificed the lamb instead, and his son was spared.

Granted, my situation with Marcee was less dramatic than Abraham's, but I felt God telling me, *I've got your back.* All I needed to do was trust Him with my time, my cousin, a blanket, a note card with the words He gave me, and the task He put before me.

Who Will God Find Faithful?

Over the years, Mitch and I have been part of generosity ministries at our church. Through these platforms, we've had the privilege to travel and speak about giving and generosity.

Oh, we've had people say, "That's easy for you. If I had lots of money, I would give too."

But I always tell them, "The key to giving is being faithful, and the moment God found me faithful was in my mom's basement—when I gave from my lack, not from an abundance."

Luke 21:1–4 tells how Jesus views gifts from the rich and the poor:

> While Jesus was in the Temple, he watched the rich people dropping their gifts in the

collection box. Then a poor widow came by and dropped in two small coins. "I tell you the truth," Jesus said, "this poor widow has given more than all the rest of them. For they have given a tiny part of their surplus, but she, poor as she is, has given everything she has."

There I was, sitting on my bed in Mom's basement, bills spread out in front of me, with only forty dollars to my name and absolutely no clue how to provide for my babies. Then I gave all the money I had to God. After that, God knew He could trust me with whatever resources He put into my hands.

The question isn't *How much are you giving?* but *Are you willing to give everything?* I could have blamed God for my lack. I could have said, *Really, God? This is how You provide?* But I just gave Him what I had, with nothing left. Then He blessed my giving. My lack made the gold of generosity shine brighter.

I feel like God is always looking down from heaven asking whom He can trust. And He's so pleased when we have a faith that risks everything, when we're willing to give everything we have.

Whatever He allows to filter through your hands, praise God. But it all belongs to Him.

Reflection Questions

- All of us sometimes feel like we don't have much to offer God. How can you be faithful with whatever He's given you?
- How could you bless God, whether with your time, your talent, or your treasures?

CHAPTER 6

FORGIVE

Our third-grade twins were getting off the school bus one day when a sixth-grade neighbor boy said to Tyler, "I've been thinking about how I'm going to kill you." And then he described what he would do in graphic detail.

This boy was a goth kid, always wearing a long, black trench coat that looked like a cape. He also knew we were Christians, and he did everything he could to make our lives miserable. He drew Satanic symbols on the pavement of our cul-de-sac. He put upside-down crosses on our mailbox and threw our mail on the ground. One time when we had a babysitter with the kids, he broke into our house.

Tyler was traumatized by what this kid said and came running home to tell me about it. This death threat was the last straw. I immediately went to his house and knocked on the door. When his mother answered, I told her what happened.

"Well, your boys just pick on my son," she said, and then she slammed the door in my face.

My third-graders pick on your sixth-grader?

From that point on, our circle drive became the cul-de-sac from hell. The mother despised us, and she caused problems for us at the school and spread rumors about us.

One day when I was reading the Bible, I started praying the words from Psalm 139:23–24: "Search me, O God, and know my heart; test me and know my anxious thoughts. Point out anything in me that offends you, and lead me along the path of everlasting life.

Instantly the Lord said, *Go ask the neighbor for forgiveness.*

My response? *What? Seriously? Ask her for forgiveness? I have no problem asking someone for forgiveness. But asking her for forgiveness? That's like implying that her actions were condoned. And what she did was so incredibly wrong and vindictive.*

But God said, *I'm not saying to ask forgiveness for something you did wrong but for offenses caused.*

Oh, okay. Offenses might have been caused even before that interaction at her door. I didn't know what they were; I just knew I had to obey.

It was a few weeks before Christmas, so I created a little Christmas gift. But since I doubted this woman would listen to anything I told her verbally, I added a heartfelt note asking her to forgive me for any offenses

I had caused her, then walked across the cul-de-sac and left the gift and note at her door.

A few minutes later, she was at my own door bawling. She wrapped her arms around me and squeezed me tightly. "No," she said. "I'm the one who needs to ask for forgiveness. I am so sorry for everything I've done to you. What I did was wrong."

We forgave each other, and from that point on, her heart changed. And she must have told her son what happened, because he transformed from the goth kid in the neighborhood to the neighborhood saint. He even brought out his leaf blower and blew leaves for everyone in our entire cul-de-sac. He shifted.

God not only spoke to me about the power of forgiveness but showed me that asking for forgiveness isn't only for when we know we've done something wrong. We don't know what's going on in the heart of the person with whom we're at odds, and even if we didn't intend to hurt them, they're still hurt.

We must always ask the Lord to search our hearts and speak to us. I would never have thought to ask this neighbor for forgiveness, but after God told me to and I did, that act of obedience changed the environment in our entire neighborhood. Ask yourself what you might have done to hurt someone who's hurt you. What might you need to take responsibility for? There's always more to the story.

Forgiving Others

The story about my neighbor illustrates asking for forgiveness. Now let's flip the coin to its other side: forgiving others.

The most important part of the process of forgiving is prayer. It's hard to hate someone you're praying for. Pray genuine blessings for the person who's hurt you. Then try to feel what they're feeling. Put yourself in their shoes. Try to see the situation from their perspective and remember that everyone is a product of their past and their circumstances. Our life experiences—and the life skills we have or have not gained—shape who we all become and how we respond to life. If people hurt us, their action can be a product of their past.

One of the greatest hindrances to people's success in life is unforgiveness. It holds us in bondage, and we can't be free to live the life God has provided. Plus, God tells us in Matthew 6:14–15, "If you forgive those who sin against you, your heavenly Father will forgive you. But if you refuse to forgive others, your Father will not forgive your sins." (Ouch.) You're stunting your growth if you can't forgive other people. Forgiveness is a key tool for spiritual growth and success in life.

But what if we think we've forgiven someone, yet we rehearse the hurtful situation in our minds over and over again, feeling emotions like sadness, anger, resentment, and bitterness rather than empathy, compassion, or peace? Then we haven't completed the process of forgiveness. We need to work on forgiveness again so we can truly release the offense. As the saying goes, bitterness is like drinking poison and expecting the other person to die.

Forgiving Yourself

We've also got to forgive ourselves. Yes, it's easier to forgive other people, but God says He's removed our sins as far as the east is from the west (Psalm 103:12). If we seek forgiveness from the Lord and believe He's forgiven us, then who are we to not free ourselves from unforgiveness?

To forgive ourselves, we've got to recognize that God forgives us even though we don't deserve it. Of course, sometimes we do wrong without meaning to, but that doesn't make a difference. The apostle Paul wrote, "I used to blaspheme the name of Christ. In my insolence, I persecuted his people. But God had mercy on me because I did it in ignorance and unbelief" (1 Timothy 1:13). Regardless of why we did wrong, we must forgive ourselves and know that God forgives us when we repent.

Forgiving Those in My Past

Even after I married Mitch, I had to be in contact with the father of my three oldest children, Shawn. Everything would be going beautifully, with me experiencing God moments and feeling amazed by everything He was doing in my life, and then Shawn would call and I would spiral downhill. I would feel worthless, like I was absolutely nothing.

I needed to forgive Shawn and let go of the past. But I knew my wounds had started before Shawn. I needed to forgive my biological father, and I needed to forgive my sister.

I met with my father and told him I forgave him for everything he'd done to me. It wasn't the conversation I hoped for. We weren't instantly friends, and he wasn't suddenly an amazing father. But the conversation wasn't bad. And afterward, I felt completely free of hurt and bitterness. Two months later, he died from heart failure. I was so grateful I had the opportunity to release him and not have to carry the guilt of withholding forgiveness or wishing I had been able to tell him I forgave him.

Then I reached out to my sister and told her I forgave her, letting go of everything in our past. She ended up visiting me, one of the few times I saw her after she left home with Chuck.

Shawn lived in California, and by this time Mitch, the kids, and I had moved to Washington. One year, Shawn wanted the kids to come to him for Thanksgiving, which happened to fall on the twins' birthday. My heart sank because I had never been apart from any of my children on their birthdays. I was praying about what to do when God told me to invite Shawn to our house for Thanksgiving.

I'm thinking, *I rebuke you, Satan.*

But I prayed, *Okay, Lord, if you say so.*

I called Mitch. "God told me we need to invite Shawn to come here for Thanksgiving."

"I agree," Mitch said. "And I think he needs to stay at our house too." *Holy cow!*

Before inviting Shawn, I talked with all the kids to ask how they felt about his joining us for the holiday. My oldest daughter, Melissa, said, "No, Mom, no. You can't do that." But she'd been memorizing Psalm 23, and suddenly she gasped, then started quoting the part where David says God prepared a feast for him in the presence of his enemies.

Then she said, "Yes, Mom, yes! He has to come here. God has prepared a table before us in the presence of our enemies. He will take care of us. Shawn has to come for Thanksgiving!"

After Melissa's instant change of heart, I thought, *Okay, Lord, this is your plan.*

I called Shawn.

"So, um, you know . . ." Starting this conversation gently was hard, so I decided to just jump in. "We were wondering if you'd like to come to our house for Thanksgiving."

He started listing all the reasons he couldn't come. For one thing, he didn't have the money.

Yes! I thought. Then silently mouthed, *Sorry, God, I tried.*

Instantly God told me, *You'll pay for it.*

Sigh. "We'll pay for you to come here," I told Shawn.

He agreed. So now my kids' dad was joining us for Thanksgiving. Fantastic.

Before Shawn came, Mitch and I realized we were expecting him to be a good father to the children even though we knew he didn't know how. We were counting on something unattainable for him. Then I thought back to the week I spent with Sherry. Maybe seeing a healthy family could help him be a better father.

The week Shawn spent at our house was a supernatural experience for us all. He went to church with us and responded to the altar call, crying out to God on his hands and knees. It was so beautiful. He was truly touched during our time with us, and I was able to completely forgive him for everything. I never regretted obeying God's command. Forgiving is one of the best things we can ever do.

Going Forward

From that experience, I learned we don't get to decide who Jesus died for. And, friend, that means Jesus died for anyone who's hurt you.

In John 21:15–16, Jesus appears to the disciples after rising from the dead. They've been out fishing, and He's made them all breakfast on the shore. After they eat, He says,

> "Simon son of John, do you love me more than these?"
>
> "Yes, Lord," Peter replied, "you know I love you."
>
> "Then feed my lambs," Jesus told him.
>
> Jesus repeated the question: "Simon son of John, do you love me?"
>
> "Yes, Lord," Peter said, "you know I love you."
>
> "Then take care of my sheep," Jesus said.

Jesus repeats the question a third time. "Do you love me?" When Peter again says he loves Him, Jesus replies, "Then feed my sheep." But He didn't mean those of us who love Him can choose whom to feed. We don't feed other people because they deserve it; we feed them because we love Jesus. It's not our role to determine who's qualified to be fed or who deserves to enter God's kingdom. Jesus brings people into His kingdom regardless of who they are or what they've done. It's just our job to feed them.

In my worst state, God chose me. And in every person's worst state, God chooses them.

I try to look at people the same way Jesus does and remember we're all going through our own journey. How we handle any hurtful situation could be a determining factor in the other person's life with Christ, and we have no idea the impact we can make by forgiving them.

Audrey's Story

If you don't forgive, the wound you've suffered controls you the rest of your life. And unforgiveness gives the people who hurt us the power to keep destroying us for the rest of their lives.

My dear friend Audrey May Prosper is a pillar of the faith and a mighty woman of God who shares her powerful story of forgiveness around the world.

She'd asked her first husband, an NYPD police officer, for a divorce for more reasons than one. Then one day after work she stopped at the home they'd once shared. He was supposed to be at jury duty, but as soon as she opened the door, he forced her into the garage and began beating her with a hammer. Then he poured gasoline all over her and set her on fire. When Audrey escaped through the garage door, a neighbor ran over, helped put out the flames, and then called an ambulance.

Audrey's life had completely changed in that moment in time. She was in a coma for six weeks, and, suffering burns over 80 percent of her body, she had many, many surgeries ahead of her.

Her husband went to prison, and she eventually divorced him.

Fast-forward ten years. Recently remarried, Audrey had forgiven her ex-husband for what he did. But she and her second husband felt like they needed to do something for him outwardly to show she'd forgiven him.

This is what happened next: Her ex-husband hadn't seen his and Audrey's two beautiful sons for a decade, so Audrey's new husband (who is absolutely amazing) took them to the prison to see their father. Audrey went with them, but she stayed in the car, and I watched her on Facebook live as she sat in the prison parking lot talking about the importance of forgiveness. Her story is one of the most incredible acts of forgiveness I've heard, and her heart reminds me of Jesus.

Even as Jesus hung on a cross, He prayed, "Father, forgive them, for they don't know what they are doing" (Luke 23:34). I look back on Audrey's life and the life of Jesus, and then I compare their lives to mine. I might have gone through hard circumstances, but I didn't have over 80 percent of my body burned. I wasn't hung on a cross. If they were able to forgive, I don't believe anything I experienced is too great for me to forgive.

Precious one, forgiveness is not an option. It's a command. Yes, forgiveness can feel like giving up, and it can be incredibly hard. People break us. They shatter us to pieces. If we keep clinging to those broken shards, though, we only keep cutting our own hands. We've got to let go and give the broken pieces to God. Then He can pick up our shattered lives and start piecing them back together, lining each jagged edge with the brilliance of His gold.

Forgiveness means giving the brokenness back to God. No matter how someone has broken us, God can put us back together. No matter how we've contributed to our own brokenness, God can put us back together better than before.

Giving Jesus Control

To truly forgive, though, we must understand the message in this story my friend Emmanuel Ziga shared with one of my sons. I've shared it with others many times since.

A man wants Jesus to come stay at his house.

"I'd be happy to," Jesus says. So the man cleans out a room, making it beautiful because he wants it to be spectacular for Jesus. Jesus moves into the house, and it's incredible. He loves being there.

Then one day there's a knock at the door. The man opens it and finds Satan. Satan rips the man out of his house and beats him to a pulp. Bloody and bruised, the man finally cries, "Jesus!"

Jesus comes running, then tears the man away from Satan's grasp and carries him back into the house. He mends his wounds, totally healing and restoring him.

A few days later, Satan returns and does the exact same thing. Again the man calls out, "Jesus!" Jesus comes running again, then pulls him back into the house and mends his wounds.

The man says, "Jesus, I don't understand. Why do I have to keep calling out to you? And why didn't you help me in the first place, protecting me from this even happening?"

"This is your home," Jesus says. "I don't have authority here; you do. I can help you only when you call on My name." Then He says, "But why don't you give this a try? Why don't you give Me your entire home and let Me take care of everything for you?"

"Anywhere with You is great, Jesus," the man says, "so sure, take my home."

Another knock comes a little later. This time Jesus opens it, and Satan drops to his knees. "Oh, I'm so sorry, I'm so sorry," he says. "I didn't know this house belongs to You." Satan never returned to that home.

We need to give the whole of our lives to Jesus. If we compartmentalize Him and call on Him only when it's convenient for us, He can't have authority; He can't reign in our lives. Only when we fully give our lives to Him can we achieve real success in life. That's when we can be free from the attacks of the Enemy.

Give Jesus your all. Don't give Him only a piece of you. He can't be just a part of your life alongside work, school, hobbies, friends, family, or anything that can divide you from Him. As Christians, we must allow Jesus to be the center of everything we do. Our work revolves around Him. Raising children and loving a spouse revolve around Him. Our social climate, the friends we hang out with—it all revolves around Him. If we make Him the center of everything we do, we'll experience success, joy, and fulfillment.

And yes, we'll truly be able to forgive.

Reflection Questions

- Seek the Lord and ask Him to show you whom you need to forgive.
- Now ask Him whom you need to seek forgiveness from.

CHAPTER 7

EXPECT MIRACLES

Years ago on a Saturday evening, Mitch and I were out for dinner with friends when I got a call from a number I didn't recognize. It was a paramedic in Portland, Oregon, where our daughter Ariel had gone to attend a conference with one of my best friends, Lisa.

"Your daughter was in an accident," the man told me calmly. (I'll tell you about the accident itself later.) Then he was as chill as could be, mentioning bumps and bruises and stitches. But because Ariel was only thirteen, we needed to be the ones to sign her out of the hospital. Lisa couldn't do it.

Mitch and I weren't too concerned as we started for Portland, but then I received a second phone call, this time from a doctor. I put him on speaker, and he sounded relaxed as well. I now know both men were just trying not to frighten us.

"We're with Ariel," he said. "We're just wondering what your timeframe is for when you'll arrive. And we wanted to let you know we're moving her to another hospital."

"Oh, okay," I said. "How is she?"

"She has a broken hand and maybe a couple of skull fractures."

Mitch and I looked at each other. Skull fractures? Mitch sped up, which of course made me more anxious. He was even tailgating and honking at other cars. Then he put on his hazards, pulled into the emergency lane, and flew down the highway. That was the shortest drive from Seattle to Portland I've ever experienced.

Lisa and I weren't exactly sure why she didn't call us. I believe she was in shock just trying to figure out what to do, or maybe it was God protecting us. I'm grateful we hadn't spoken prior to seeing her at the hospital. I think it would have been warp speed then.

"We're here to see our daughter, Ariel Soule," I said to a nurse when we arrived at the hospital.

"You can't see her right now. You need to wait for the caseworker."

A caseworker? I thought. *Aren't they called in for suspected abuse?* We weren't even in the state we lived in. Then I realized the caseworker wasn't there for Ariel. They were there for us. My heart sank.

"But she's alone," we said. "She needs us."

Mitch and I waited for what seemed like forever, and when the doctor and caseworker finally joined us, they had a stack of papers an inch and a half thick.

How can they even have all this paperwork on her already? I thought. *She just entered.*

They showed us X-ray and CT pictures of her skull. They slid the picture over to us and turned it so it was facing us. The whole right side of her face was completely crushed, and her eye was down where her cheek should have been.

They started listing her injuries. A crushed hand. A bruised lung. A cracked skull. A shattered face. And she had a brain bleed. Then the doctor said, "We don't know if she's going to live. But if she does, she will likely be a vegetable."

That day in 2012, we clung to every ounce of faith in us! After all, we'd seen God heal in our family before, and we were sure He could do it again. I thought back to our past stories of healing.

The Cure for Asthma

One Sunday morning when Ariel was two, Melissa was in fourth grade, and the boys were in second grade, we were running late for church. Now, Mitch is very punctual and hates running late, but by the time we got everyone out the door, we knew we wouldn't arrive on time.

"Why don't we go to a different church?" I said.

I meant a church in the same denomination, but Mitch drove us to a church from a different denomination. It was also huge, with thousands of people. At our church, our kids were 50 percent of the youth group, and the congregation was losing members because they were so elderly and dying off.

Not only was this church huge but it was charismatic. *This is weird*, I thought. But there we were.

At the end of the service, the pastor, Pastor Wendell, gave an altar call for healing. Now, both our twins had been born with severe asthma, and Tyler's was so severe that if he had an attack, we just took him to the hospital as fast as we could. His oxygen levels would plummet, and medical personnel could hardly get them back up. He'd just recently been in the hospital for five days, and his levels were still susceptible to lowering again.

I was kind of freaked out, but I decided to take both boys to the altar.

When Pastor Wendell put his hands on them, he chuckled a little. It was the sweetest, gentlest chuckle I'd ever heard. Then he prayed a beautiful prayer over both Tyler and Dylan.

When we got home, I immediately started to prepare a nebulizer treatment for Tyler. But he said, "No, Mom. I'm healed!"

"That's great, buddy," I told him. "But you need this treatment." He was seven, and while it was sweet to see his faith, I wasn't ready for another trip to the hospital.

"No. I'm healed!"

I didn't want to stomp on his budding faith, but I had a sick kid to take care of. "That's great," I said again, "but you still need to do what the doctors say."

"No. You took me up there, and that man prayed for me. I'm healed."

"How do you know?"

"When he prayed, I felt tingling in my chest, like a boa constrictor was wrapped around me. Then it got really hot on my head, and the heat went all the way down my body. Then it all just went away."

What do you say to that? I didn't administer the treatment. Instead, I took out his peak flow meter, which measures how well the air moves out of the lungs. The reading was perfect. I checked again after fifteen minutes, then after half an hour, then after an hour, and so on.

We decided to keep going to that church.

Tyler never had another asthma attack. The doctors had claimed he'd never outgrow his asthma because his lungs were permanently damaged. He'd never be able to play sports, they said. But he became a star athlete, and now he's in his twenties, still completely healed.

Dylan was healed too.

The twins' healing was such a profound moment for us. For the first time, we saw God as a miracle-healing God. I'd had such a naive faith. But after that experience, and with a huge faith, I lived with an expectation for healing.

A New Life

As our kids grew older, God told Mitch we weren't done having kids. After praying, I was in agreement, so we both had medical procedures to allow us to have another baby.

Long story short, I got pregnant six times only to miscarry. At a certain point, I went on bed rest as soon as I thought I could be pregnant again. Then if we found out I wasn't pregnant, I went off bed rest. If we found out I was pregnant, I stayed on bed rest—only to miscarry.

This went on for more than two years. Many months I was out of bed for only two weeks before I was back again.

The first miscarriage was heartbreaking. Then when I got pregnant a second time, we thought, *Look at God's redemption. He is so faithful. He is so good.* Then I lost the second one.

After the third miscarriage, I was crushed. My faith was shattered. I prayed, *God, why would this happen? You told Mitch we weren't done. Then we went through those medical procedures only to lose our babies.*

A few days later, I went to church on Sunday morning, and Pastor Jude was preaching. In the middle of his sermon, he stopped and said, "Christine Soule. Please come forward. I have a word for you." I just sat there, stunned. Then he said again, "Come forward."

Now, I had never seen such a thing at church, nor have I seen anything like it since. But I made my way to the front of the sanctuary, and the pastor walked down the stage steps to meet me.

"I have a word for you," he said. "What you've been desiring, you will have within the week." Then Jude turned around and walked back up the steps.

I stood there thinking, *Excuse me?* But he was preaching again, so I returned to my seat and prayed.

Seriously, God. What I've been desiring? I just miscarried again. I am so broken from this. And You're saying I'll have what I'm desiring within the week? That's not even physically possible.

But on Wednesday I took a pregnancy test, and it read positive.

I called my doctor, Dr. Lawler, who had just walked me through my third miscarriage, and told him the news. He's a Christian, and I also told him what Jude said.

"Christine, you are not pregnant. You still have pregnancy hormones in your body from the last baby.

Your body is going crazy, and your hormones are out of whack, so a pregnancy test is going to read positive. But that doesn't mean you're pregnant."

"Yeah, but—"

"I'll tell you what. Wait a week. Do another test. If it reads positive, come see me."

The test a week later read positive as well. So I went to see him, and sure enough, I was pregnant.

"This isn't possible," he said. "You had a D and C, meaning I scraped out the lining of your uterus. There was nothing left there. And this can't be a twin or anything like that. A twin couldn't survive a D and C."

I hadn't had a period since then, so there was also no way another egg would have been released. But somehow, I was pregnant. Now here's the crazy part: I was nine weeks pregnant when I miscarried the last baby, but this one was about four weeks along. Yet with all the 4D ultrasounds done by a neonatologist, we hadn't seen it.

We named our fifth child, our third daughter, Zoë, which means life.

Hard Things

As we sat listening to that caseworker, I tried to envision my baby girl's future. *Would I see her graduate from school? Would her dad walk her down the aisle toward*

*the man who would be her husband? Would I get to see her
with babies?*

I suddenly felt like I was going to faint. I don't know
if anything can really prepare you to hear that your child
might not live. But from previous experience, I knew
God could heal Ariel. Over and over, I'd seen Him come
through for our family, and I knew He could do the
impossible.

This is what happened to Ariel the day of her accident.

My wonderful friend Lisa had driven her three
daughters, Ariel, and another friend to this conference in
Portland hosted by the authors of the book for teenagers
titled *Do Hard Things*. At the conference, the speakers
inspired the youth to be bold. Their message went
something like this: "As a young person, you can do great
things for the Lord. You don't have to sit back and wait.
You can see what God has for you now."

When the conference ended, Lisa drove everyone to
her brother's house, and this is what she later relayed to us.

It was a warm summer Saturday in July, and the
kids were having fun riding four-wheelers and dirt bikes
around her brother's property in the country and down
a quiet road. Lisa was sitting on the steps of the front
porch when her nephew and one of her daughters pulled
into the driveway in their four-wheeler. At the same
time, Ariel was riding a dirt bike, going in the opposite
direction.

They collided. Ariel flew off her bike and sailed over the top of the four-wheeler, then landed on concrete. Lisa saw the collision and Ariel's helmet flying off (it hadn't been strapped on), but she couldn't see Ariel's landing.

When she ran to her, Ariel was lying on her face. There was some blood, and she wasn't talking.

Oh, Jesus, Lisa prayed. *Be with her. Help her.*

She yelled for someone to call nine-one-one, then stayed by Ariel, holding her and praying for her. Later, Ariel recalled going in and out of consciousness and attempting to communicate but to no avail. When Lisa got on the phone with the nine-one-one dispatcher, she was asked if Ariel had a heartbeat. Lisa checked. None. Could she feel Ariel breathing? No.

The ambulance arrived, and after the paramedics stabilized Ariel enough that they could transport her, they whisked her to the hospital.

Later, Ariel's hand revealed one of the first miracles. As she was falling, Ariel realized her helmet was coming off, so she reached up to pull it back on. That meant her hand hit the ground before her face. The impact crushed her whole hand, but the doctors told us that move probably saved her life.

She was asleep when Mitch and I were finally allowed to see her. I almost passed out, and the nurses had to catch me. Ariel's face was so disfigured, and I was sure she would never look the same. I accepted that.

Then at one point her neck started swelling, and we were told she might need a tracheotomy, which meant cutting a hole in her throat for a breathing tube. If they did that, they said, her voice would never be the same.

I almost passed out again. Even as a thirteen-year-old, Ariel was a singer and songwriter. That was what she loved.

I thought back to when she was five years old and we took her to Tommy Barnett's church, the LA Dream Center. Pastor Tommy delivered a powerful message, and at the end of the night, he asked, "Has God spoken to anyone here tonight?"

Sitting on her daddy's lap, little Ariel raised her hand. Tommy smiled and walked down to her with the microphone.

"Honey, has God spoken something to you?"

"Yes."

"What did He say?"

"I'm going to be a singer for Jesus."

"Can you sing?"

"Oh, yes."

"Here, sing something," Tommy said, handing her the mic. Tommy leaned over, expecting her to sing something right there. But no, not my daughter. She jumped off Mitch's lap and marched up to the center of the stage.

She'd been practicing a song for a Fourth of July parade, and so in front of thousands of people, my five-year-old daughter belted out "Proud to Be an American," a cappella. The crowd loved it, and she'd never stopped singing.

Now here we were in a hospital room eight years later, being told she might never be able to sing again if she had this procedure. So we started praying. Lisa called people from the church and asked them all to start praying. They all passed the word around, and then thousands of people were praying. Ariel was supposed to have attended summer camp by then, and the whole camp—including thousands of kids—were all praying for her too.

Soon the swelling went down, and she never needed the tracheotomy. Later, when I heard the voice of an angel coming from her once again, I lost it! That's still one of the most beautiful sounds I've ever heard.

Healing Against All Odds

I spent the first night in Ariel's hospital room. She hadn't spoken since the accident, but in the middle of the night, she said, "Grandpa."

Her grandpa had just died a few months earlier. I jumped up and said, "Don't go into the light. Don't go into the light." It was all I could think of, but what would you have said?

Ariel needed multiple surgeries. One was to reconstruct her face and lift her eye back up into its socket. Another was to remove shattered bone fragments from her face. When her cheekbone shattered, the fragments became like shards of glass embedded in her muscle tissue. The surgery to remove them was high stakes. If the doctor missed any of the pieces, every time Ariel smiled or talked, she would feel those "shards of glass" poking her, and she would live with that pain indefinitely. But if they did the surgery with a CAT scan machine in the room, the surgeon would be able to see every little bit of bone particle and remove them all.

Only five CAT scan machines small enough to fit in a room during surgery were in the United States, and they traveled between hospitals. Yet one of them was already there. The surgeon was amazed and so grateful to have that tool available. What's more, he was the pioneer who created the new surgery technique of cutting from the inside of the mouth rather than from the outside of the face. This new procedure protected Ariel from further scarring. We could not have been more blessed.

As they were wheeling her off to the first surgery, she kept asking me to say her good-byes to different people that meant a lot to her. She wasn't sure if she'd come out of surgery that day, but she came out of every single one.

Eventually she was released from the hospital, even with a brain bleed still present. The doctors thought it had stopped growing and she'd be okay. So when Ariel wanted to go to church on Sunday, we dropped her off at her youth group meeting and headed into the service. Then somebody came for us, saying Ariel wasn't feeling well. She was dizzy and was hearing sounds and seeing changes in her vision.

"We're taking you to Harborview," we said. Harborview is a level-one trauma center in Seattle, serving four states. They often life-flight people there, but we lived fairly close by. They did a CAT scan of her brain and saw that the brain bleed had in fact grown exponentially. It was two and a half times the size their protocol dictates operating. Next thing we knew, Ariel was in critical condition in the ICU again. And they told us that to do the brain surgery, they'd have to remove a six-by-four portion of her skull.

Ariel didn't bat an eye—until they told her they'd have to shave her head. Then she shed a tear. What thirteen-year-old girl wants to be bald?

When eight neurosurgeons walked in, Ariel said hi to them.

The head doctor stared at her, then said, "Oh, I'm so sorry. We must have the wrong room." He picked up her chart and studied it, then asked, "Are you Ariel?"

"Yeah, that's me."

The surgeons looked at each other, apparently baffled.

They explained that with a brain bleed as large as hers, Ariel should have been dead. Or at the very least, completely unconscious with no neurological function. Instead, they found an alert thirteen-year-old with a headache. They decided to postpone the surgery until morning.

But the next morning the head surgeon told her, "I just don't feel like I can do this surgery today, not when you seem to be doing as well as you are." However, by that night, they felt so uncomfortable with the size of the brain bleed that they decided to do the surgery the next day. "We've got to relieve the pressure," they said. "We've got to do this."

The next morning they ran test after test, but after communicating with Ariel, who was functioning just fine, they put off the surgery again.

This continued for days. They couldn't bear to let the swelling continue to put pressure on her brain, but they also couldn't bring themselves to do surgery when she was defying all odds.

They even asked Mitch and me what we thought they should do. I looked at eight neurosurgeons and said, "Please don't ask me that question."

The doctors were phenomenal. We were sitting in the children's waiting room next to a fish tank one day, and one of the neurosurgeons, white-haired, came in to talk with us personally.

"I can't even believe it," he kept exclaiming. "She should be a vegetable. This isn't possible."

Each of the eight doctors came to us privately and said Ariel was a miracle. None of them would admit it in a group, but one by one they told us the same thing. They couldn't believe what they were seeing.

Our family has a philosophy: if the devil takes us to the hospital, we're going to make him pay. God heals, and we believe if He hasn't healed someone *yet*, that probably means someone involved still needs Jesus. This was definitely true in this case. We had opportunity after opportunity to share the gospel while Ariel was in Harborview. Always the songwriter, Ariel wrote a song while she was there. Then she walked up and down the hall, going from room to room, singing it to her fellow patients.

As her parent, I had meetings with all sorts of people about her condition. I had no idea the hospital had so many counselors and therapists for every aspect of her treatment. One warned me she might never be the same. She had landed on her right frontal lobe, the part of the brain that regulates how we express emotions, so they said she could experience ongoing anger, even rage. She might need to be institutionalized.

But one day I looked at her singing to a patient across the hall, and said to the medical professional with me, "Nope. The accident just knocked her nicer."

Then they brought in a psychologist to talk to me. He said the same thing, trying to help me understand that my daughter would never be the same. But I insisted this was wrong. "Nope, the accident just knocked her nicer," I declared. I wanted to speak life over her.

Just think about it. When God says "death and life are in the power of the tongue" in Proverbs 18:21 (NKJV), He's not joking, friend! Speak life over your circumstances. And James 1:6–7 says anyone whose faith is not in God alone "should not expect to receive anything from the Lord." Have you ever prayed for something, then turned around and doubted or worried that it wouldn't happen? We felt we had no other option but to believe for a total miracle. The book of Job says the very thing Job feared came upon him. Unwavering faith in God was our only option.

In Romans 4:17–22, Paul talks about Abraham's faith. He writes,

> This happened because Abraham believed in the God who brings the dead back to life and who creates new things out of nothing. Even when there was no reason for hope, Abraham kept hoping. … [His] faith did not weaken. … Abraham never wavered in believing God's promise. In fact, his faith grew stronger, and in this he brought glory to God. He was fully convinced that God is able to do whatever he promises. And because of Abraham's faith, God counted him as righteous.

How do we find righteousness in God? By being faithful. In verse 24, Paul writes, "God will also count us as righteous if we believe in Him." We just need to keep believing. As Abraham got older, his hope of being the father of many nations grew dimmer, yet his faith grew stronger. He was fully convinced that God would do whatever He promised. That's our stand too. As believers, we must be convinced that God will do what He promised He would do. We have got to keep believing. The broken parts of life teach us faith.

Healing Delayed

Although God has the power to prevent illness and injury, sometimes He chooses not to.

In John 9, John writes, "As [Jesus] went along, he saw a man blind from birth. His disciples asked him, 'Rabbi, who sinned, this man or his parents, that he was born blind?' 'Neither this man nor his parents sinned,' said Jesus, 'but this happened so that the works of God might be displayed in him'" (John 9:1–3 NIV).

Sometimes, then, God allows sickness or injury so His glory will be displayed. This man was born blind not because he had done something wrong but so Jesus could heal him!

Many doctors witnessed a miracle with Ariel, and our family saw countless miracles as we shared Jesus with other patients. Sometimes, though, the miracles come slowly; God allows a learning process, letting us discover how to trust our Abba Father, our Papa.

Healing God's Way

One day a man walked into Ariel's room in tears.

"Can we help you?" I asked.

He struggled to gain composure, then said, "You don't know me, but my daughter was with your daughter in Portland when she had the accident, and she's been updating us on Ariel's progress. My other daughter was once in this very room. I know it was this room because I work across the street, and I could see her window from my office. Every day I begged God for a miracle. That miracle never came, and God took my daughter home." He paused before continuing. "But Ariel is the miracle I was hoping for. Thank you. Your faith has restored mine."

Beloved, I don't know why God chose to restore our precious Ariel and not that man's daughter, at least not here on earth. I'm sure he believed. But I do know we can always trust God's promises. We just can't control His process.

The Neurosurgeon Convention

Ariel never needed that brain surgery. It was a total miracle. In fact, she's in medical books now. None of the doctors had ever seen a brain bleed that large that didn't require surgery. In 2013, the president of Harborview asked if we could share her story at the forty-year anniversary of the Society for Neuroscience in Anesthesiology and Critical Care. In their entire history, Ariel was the first patient they'd asked to be a speaker. Harborview's president, a woman, told us asking her was a risk as well, because the profession was dominated by men. Neurosurgery was a man's world.

Ariel and I flew to DC to be panelists at the convention, attended by eight hundred neurosurgeons. They seemed very staunch and stoic as they sat in the audience. Several neurosurgeons shared their latest discoveries, then it was our turn. I shared my experience, and then Ariel shared hers. Ariel ended her story with the song she'd written for the ICU patients.

As she sang, many of the neurosurgeons wiped away tears. After the presentations, doctors lined the aisle for their turn to ask a question. Every single one was for Ariel or me. A room full of eight hundred neurosurgeons, and all their questions were directed to me or my now fourteen-year-old daughter. No one in the audience could comprehend how her case was possible.

One of them wanted to write about Ariel in his book. Another doctor offered her a full-ride medical scholarship. Ariel told that doctor, "No thank you. I'm going to be a singer." And of course, as her encouraging mother, I kicked her under the table and whispered, "Plan B?"

"Mom," she whispered back. "You know I'm never going to be a doctor." Funny thing is, she's going to school now to be a counselor. Hmm. But that scholarship would have been nice. Ha ha!

You see, we expected miracles when Ariel was injured. We started our relationship with the Holy Spirit when our boys were healed of their asthma, and we believed God could and would do more. And He does. Crazy, I know!

We've always told our kids if we ever need hospitalization, it will no doubt be because someone there needs Jesus. We'll go with our eyes wide open and our hearts ready to hear what the Holy Spirit has to say about how He wants us to share the glory of God with others.

Reflection Questions

○—▪ What do you believe about healing? How has God healed you or someone you love in the past?

○—▪ Do you still need healing today? If so, who can you ask to pray for you? What are your next steps going to be in believing for that miracle?

CHAPTER 8

KNOW YOUR TRUE NEW IDENTITY

I talked about knowing our true identity in the preface of this book, but now let's unpack this foundational must for us all.

My mother sat across from me at our favorite restaurant, and as we picked up our forks to dig into the steaming goodness, she said, "I really shouldn't be eating this meal; I'm so fat."

Now, I love my mom. She really is one of my heroes. She's gone through so much and has completely risen above it. But when she was a kid, her parents called her "elephant legs." They thought it was a funny nickname. Can you imagine growing up with that being spoken over you? Remember, God says death and life are in the power of the tongue. Of course she saw herself as fat! She felt unworthy, as though she was never enough.

My mom was always so kind to me as I grew up. She never said anything negative about my body, which I'm so thankful for. But I listened to the way she spoke about herself in front of the mirror, and I took it in as truth. Mom has the perfect body, but as I heard her critique herself, I thought, *If that's fat, what am I? I must be huge.*

When my oldest daughter, Melissa, was four, she came running up to me with a piece of paper.

"Mommy, Mommy, I have something for you!" She was just learning to read and write.

"What is it?" I said.

"It's a number! This lady said she wants to help you!"

She had written 1-800-Jenny (an ad for a popular weight-loss program).

I realized I was doing the same thing my mom had. I was complaining about how fat I was, and my sweet little girl was picking it up. The pattern had to end somewhere, and I wanted it to end with me.

That night at the restaurant, I looked my tiny, beautiful mom in the eyes and said, "You're right."

"Excuse me?"

"You're right, Mom," I repeated. "You shouldn't eat that meal. In fact, did you look at yourself in the mirror before you left the house? I can't believe you would even wear that outfit." I continued to recount just how huge she was. By the time I finished, tears flowed from her eyes.

"That is the worst thing anyone has ever said to me in my entire life," she told me.

"No, Mom," I said, "it's not. Because that's the exact thing you've told yourself my entire life. Those are the words I heard you speak over yourself day after day. Why is it acceptable for you to say them every day of your life if it's unacceptable for someone else to say them to you?"

Since that day, my mom has made a conscious choice to stop criticizing herself. Her efforts have meant so much to me, because as a result, she's taught me how to be confident with myself. And I have promised never to say such negative things about myself in front of my daughters because I don't want them to grow up believing those lies about themselves. I want them to be confident in who they are.

Body image speaks to a deep part of our identity as women, but I think God made us this way. He made us to be desirable. He made us beautiful. But when this part of our identity is broken, it can take a toll on every area of our lives. Sometimes we have to let go of what we think shapes our identity to allow God to speak a new identity over us. We have to expose the cracks in us before He can fill them in with His gold.

Identity is such a big deal today, but God knows who we are from the start. In Jeremiah 29:11, He said to the exiles in Babylon and to us, "I know the plans that I have for you . . . plans to prosper you and not to harm you, plans to give you hope and a future" (NIV). Psalm 139 says God knits us together in our mother's womb, and He knows each of our days before we're ever born. Isaiah 64:8 says, "We are the clay, you are the potter; we are all the work of your hand" (NIV). God created each of us exactly how He wanted us to be.

But then words get spoken over us, and those words become our identity. Sometimes lies are spoken over us. We can become confused. It's okay to question who we are. Even in our forties and fifties we're still discovering who God made us to be. And it's okay to go through that discovery process. But we've got to be sure we're listening to God, not to the world. Not to society. The world and society help shape us, but we must always ask, *Who does God desire me to be?*

You Are Who God Intends

As a student, I started playing around with the spelling of my name—Christine became Krystine, Kristine, Crystine. I would go by Chris, Kristin, Chrissy, Chrystal. You name it, I did it, and I was searching for who I was. By the time I turned sixteen, I had landed on Kristine, and then I went by that spelling for years because I got my first driver's license with that spelling. I didn't even think twice about whether that was legal, and apparently they didn't look at my birth certificate. Then I ended up with everything I owned—cars, credit cards—under the name Kristine.

Years later, one of our pastors mentioned us in a book he'd written. When he gave us a copy, I saw he'd spelled my name Christine.

I was like, *Hey, he spelled my name wrong.*

Right away, the Holy Spirit said, *No, he didn't.*

That took me aback. Instantly, I had this memory of my father when I was a child. It's one of the few memories I have of him, and the only fond memory. My siblings were laughing at me because I didn't have a middle name. They said I wasn't important enough to have one.

I asked my dad why he and mom hadn't given me a middle name, and he said, "Well, when we knew you were going to be born in December, we decided to name you after Jesus Christ. And then when we decided to name you after Jesus Christ, we knew no other name was needed."

In that moment, I realized my identity was in my name all along. "Christine" means follower of Christ. That is the greatest destiny I can fulfill—to follow Him and draw His people to Him. That blew my mind.

I went back to the original spelling, which was incredibly difficult. The government let me change the spelling of my name without a problem, but it was like the end of the world trying to switch it back.

Years later, though, when I finally had a credit card with my original name spelling, I took it out to pay for something. The friend I was with looked down at my card and said, "That's kind of funny. Have you ever noticed this about your name?" She covered the ine in my first name—Christine—and the e in my last name—Soule. Then she said, "Look at that. It says Christ and Soul. It's kind of like that Scripture, to love the Lord your God with all your heart and soul, and to love your neighbor as yourself. You love Christ, and you love souls." It blew my mind, because loving like that is my life calling.

My favorite Scripture in the entire Bible is Luke 10:27, and here's why: A scribe has just asked Jesus what he should do to inherit eternal life, and Jesus asks him what the Law says. In answer, the scribe draws from Deuteronomy 6:5 and Leviticus 19:18: "'You must love the LORD your God with all your heart, all your soul, all your strength, and all your mind.' And "Love your neighbor as yourself.'"

When I read that, I thought, *Yes, Jesus. That's the most important part.* And not just so I'll live eternally with God. If I could encapsulate the entire Word of God in one sentence, it would be "Love God and love His people." If we could all figure that out, we'll have solved every problem in the entire world. I am passionate about that, and the *Christ* and *Soul* in my name are my identity!

When we start to understand who we are and who we're called to be in Christ, we can begin to walk in that authority and in the calling God has for us. Only then can we truly find fulfillment in our lives and circumstances.

The Image We Believe

Growing up, my whole world revolved around what I looked like. With my dad having affairs and my mom's husbands having affairs and then working in clubs with men who were constantly having affairs . . . well, I knew early you couldn't just be pretty to get and keep a man. You had to be the prettiest girl, or the next girl would win.

And as an adult, every aspect of my past life had taught me to depend on how I looked and to fiercely protect my appearance at all costs. My world was still defined by men who committed adultery and did horrible things. I was a dancer in a strip club. And living in this environment, my worth, my value, my significance came from my appearance. Where I fit in was based on how I looked. I always felt I was in competition with other women.

Even now that I'm in my forties and happily married to the love of my life, I still too often feel like I need to compete with twenty-year-olds. Will my body ever be enough?

I'm tired of it. I'm tired of competing with much younger women. Tired of feeling insecure. Tired of feeling like I'm not enough. But it's so easy to yearn for the body we want.

Can you relate to this? You might think you look fine, but then something spoken over you sticks with you your entire life. Somebody could say you have a big nose, and oh no, now you have a huge nose. My mom was called Elephant Legs, and from then on, she thought she was fat. When I was young, a boy told me I had hairy legs. From his one comment, I thought I was the hairiest beast ever. Even as an adult, I still believed I was hairy.

Then I was talking with a friend, who honestly was hairy. I said, "Oh yeah, I'm super hairy."

"Would you look at yourself?" she said.

"Well, yeah, I mean look." I held my arm up next to hers and realized you could hardly see any wisps of hair on my arm. "I'm really not hairy, am I?"

I had been deceived. Yet I completely believed what I'd been told.

The Image We Want

I was recently talking with one of my friends, a gorgeous young African American woman. I'm talking absolutely beautiful. I shared with her, "It's exhausting trying to look like a twenty-year-old."

"Are you kidding me?" she said. "It's exhausting trying to be a white woman."

"Why would you want to be a white woman?"

She shared a story from when she was eight years old. Her class at school was doing a project, and they had to work in twos. She was paired with a little boy who took one look at her and said, "I'm not doing a project with you."

"Well, why not?" she said.

"Because you're black. I won't do anything with you."

Until that point, she had been oblivious to prejudice because of her color. But from that moment on, all she wanted was to not just look like a white woman but to be a white woman.

Why do we women want what we don't have? We compare ourselves to other women, then feel worthless because we don't look like we think we should. However we look, we wish we looked different. If we have brown hair, we want to be a blonde. If we're a blonde, we want brown hair. If we're tall, we want to be short. If we're short, we want to be tall. If we're dark, we want to be light, and if we're light, we want to be dark.

Feeling beautiful has little to do with our actual bodies. I was in competitive fitness, and even when I had only 7 percent body fat, I still felt fat! Are you kidding me? What does it take to feel skinny? I was in perfect condition, yet I still picked myself apart in front of the mirror. Our identity will never come from a percentage. No matter how hard we try to measure up, it will never be enough for us.

Masterpiece

We receive the lies we speak over ourselves and allow them to be embedded into our souls. We let them become our identity instead of looking at our identity in Christ. Yet one day, as I was feeling all the unworthiness, God brought me to Ephesians 2:10: "We are God's masterpiece."

What is a masterpiece? I wondered. I Googled the definition and read, "The artist's greatest work."

I'm God's masterpiece? My mind was blown yet again. I'm some of God's greatest work. He calls me His masterpiece.

Think about it. God calls me, Christine Soule, His masterpiece. All four feet ten inches of me is exactly how He wanted me to be. My eye color, my skin color, my height—all of it is exactly as He wanted. So why would I want to change that? God created the sunrise, the mountains, the flowers, the birds, and then He made mankind, calling us His masterpiece. And yet we want to change ourselves! We act like we're not good enough even though He considers us His masterpiece?

Precious one, every inch of you is a masterpiece.

I felt so humbled by His goodness when I read that verse. If He thinks so highly of us, why shouldn't we think that highly of ourselves?

In Romans 9:20 Paul makes this point: "Who are you, a mere human being, to argue with God? Should the thing that was created say to the one who created it, 'Why have you made me like this?'"

We have a creator. Who are we to argue with God about the way He created us to be? Short, tall, light, dark—we are His masterpieces. Every single one of us.

Recently Mitch and I visited the Louvre in Paris. I was so excited to see the Mona Lisa. But when we walked into the room that housed the painting, I thought, *Hmm, it's this itty-bitty painting on this great big wall? Seriously?* Everyone was looking at it in amazement, but I said out loud, "So what's the big deal?" Then someone told me that no matter where onlookers stand, the woman in the painting is always looking right at them. Now that was awesome.

Sometimes people can look at a masterpiece and at first, like me, fail to see its worth. Yet our creator knew exactly how precious each person would be. Beloved, you are one of a kind, handcrafted in His image, just the way He wants you. A beautiful, priceless masterpiece. But here's the deal. Others won't see your worth if you don't discover it for yourself.

We recently had an event at our house with Bill High, the genius who got me started writing a book. (Thanks, Bill!) He was doing a Legacy planning conference. By the time we finished, every couple in the room had created mission, vision, and value statements for their family. This blew my mind! (I know. I say this a lot, but it's true!) We as Christian parents do everything we can to raise our children to seek and serve the Lord. We want them to grow up with integrity and family values. Yet so often our kids don't make the choices we hope for. Why is that? We know God's Word is the true north and compass for our lives, but in the midst of that, our kids can get caught up in life and change course.

We sat there in a room full of godly Christians who'd raised their kids well, yet all but one family had kids with very hard stories. The parents who didn't had established mission, vision, and value when their children were young. Well, here's the thing about mission, vision, and values for your family: they tell your children who they are. Not everyone has that guidance. My mom was called Elephant Legs; I was told I was a hairy beast.

Life is so confusing, but those kids whose parents established their family with mission, vision, and values had a bull's-eye on their identity. Then as arrows shot out of their parents' quiver, the kids knew exactly where they were heading.

As I mentioned earlier, the Bible tells us that without vision, the people perish. Let's be people of intention. Let's have a plan and a trajectory for where our kids need to go, and then let's speak that identity into their lives.

Speak the Right Words

All you precious ones, as we go through struggles, what is spoken over us helps determine our identity. Unfortunately, our minds can be the devil's playground when we allow them to be. But when we resist him and hold our thoughts captive to make them obedient to God (2 Corinthians 10:5), we can overcome. We can become everything God desires us to be.

James 1:13–18 says,

> Let no one say when he is tempted, "I am
> tempted by God"; for God cannot be

tempted by evil, nor does He Himself tempt anyone. But each one is tempted when he is drawn away by his own desires and enticed. Then, when desire has conceived, it gives birth to sin; and sin, when it is full-grown, brings forth death. Do not be deceived, my beloved brethren. Every good gift and every perfect gift is from above, and comes down from the Father of lights, with whom there is no variation or shadow of turning. Of His own will He brought us forth by the word of truth, that we might be a kind of firstfruits of His creatures. (NKJV)

A lot of people living in sin say, "God made me this way." No, He didn't. And He never tempts anyone to live outside His will. Yet here's the truth: we are all tempted just the same. Every one of us.

In the Bible, James says we're tempted because we're drawn away by our own desires and enticed. When tempting thoughts enter our heads, we start entertaining them. Then we can become entrenched in wrong thinking. That's why we must take hold of our thoughts and the way we project our feelings. If we don't, James warns us about what comes next: "Then, when desire has conceived, it gives birth to sin; and sin, when it is full-grown, brings forth death" (verse 15).

The progression starts with thoughts. Thoughts come from our own thinking or from what people speak over us, and then we start believing what people say about us and what we think about ourselves.

We can all easily slip into entertaining wrong thoughts that then become sin. For instance, whether it involves pornography, adultery, or even a married couple going further in their sex life than God would want them to, we can all fall into the trap of sexual sin. Every one of us. No one is immune. It's a matter of holding your thoughts captive.

Here's another example: Alcoholics Anonymous is amazing, and I love it. And the Celebrate Recovery program has done so much good working with those addicted to alcohol and drugs. But if all you're thinking is I'm an addict, you're declaring something over your life that isn't true when God has delivered you.

The Word of God says, "If the Son sets you free [from sin], you will be free indeed" (John 8:36 NIV). I'm not an addict, even though I did drugs. I used to be an addict, but God delivered me and set me free. (Recall my story in chapter 3 about how God allowed me to throw away my drugs and never be tempted by drugs and alcohol again.)

Do you see the difference? *One—I'm an addict—* was my past identity; the other—*I was an addict*—is true of me today. I'm not what I used to be. Christ has made me a new creation with a new identity. It's really a matter of not accepting my old identity any longer, not allowing the Enemy to keep speaking the past over my life as if it were still true of me. Not allowing myself to speak those words. It's about rising above and overcoming.

So, beloved, search the Word of God. Pray. Resist the devil and he will flee. When thoughts that could lead to sin come in, raise up a standard. Don't buy into what the world says. Overcome the world by speaking life over yourself and those around you.

Sexual Orientation

I can't possibly do full justice to the topic of sexual orientation here—it's too complex and hot-button an issue. Book after entire book has been written about it. But it's also so relevant, and it's such a source of pain, rejection, struggle, anger, and misunderstanding between the LGBTQ community and non-gay Christians, that I can't simply pass it by. So I'll do my best to address it briefly and, I hope, redemptively. I've done my best to find the right words, but this is not my area of expertise. So please give me grace, just as I give you grace. We're both works in progress. If anything I share offends you or fails to capture your reality, just skip this and the next section. I'd rather you do that than miss the far broader message of this book.

I have close friends who are gay, and I love them dearly. They are precious and valuable, complete people—gifted, interesting, caring, broken, strong, loving, worthy of respect, with stories to tell that deserve to be heard. As with any of us, my gay friends are not problems to be fixed. They are fun, tenderhearted, creative, protective, accepting, and supportive, and the value they place on hospitality and community is something the church at large can admire and learn from.

Each one of us, however we identify sexually, is on a path of learning what our true identity is, and we continue to grow into it. We are all flawed, questing, and imperfect in so many ways. No person is less-than. We are all searching. We are all on a journey.

My Personal Journey

Growing up, I went to twelve different schools. Within about the first two weeks at any of them, I knew who fit in, who didn't fit in, and how I could be part of the popular crowd. In fifth and sixth grades, I attended a school where drugs were cool, and being really rowdy and rebellious was cool. So I started doing drugs. In fact, I was intimidating, and people thought

I would beat them up. They actually called me Mighty Midget, and they were terrified of me. The funny part is, I never laid hands on anyone, but everyone thought I would.

Education wasn't a value for kids at that school. But at the next one, it was cool to be smart. People were popular if they did well in academics. So what did I do? I went from a D and F student to a straight A and B student. It wasn't about my intelligence. It was about something deeper. But stay with me.

At my next school, in eighth grade, athletes and gymnasts were popular. I had never done gymnastics before, but I became a gymnast. Gymnastics turned out to be a great passion of mine. I was good at it, and I really loved it. Then I injured myself and was no longer able to do gymnastics. But if I wasn't a gymnast, then who was I?

When I got my first period, I was in a tree with boys, and I wished I were a boy! Let's face it, ladies, getting our periods is no picnic. I think every girl wishes she were a boy at that moment, but that doesn't make her a boy. I was rough and tough when I was a kid, and I liked to do very masculine things—a girl who liked doing guy stuff.

But I was also a girl who, growing up, experienced terrible abuse from men, including my own stepfather. And that didn't change when I became a young woman and then a single mom, working as a stripper to support myself and my three little children. After I was raped, I hated men. After all I'd been through with them—the lack of love, the emotional and physical abuse, the depersonalization—becoming a lesbian just made sense. And I liked it. That's who I was, or at least thought I was—my identity, and I embraced it.

You read the rest of my story earlier. When I put my life in Jesus's hands, He changed a lot about me instantly, including that aspect of me. But let me be very clear that this was my experience. I'm not implying it should be yours. You have your own story, and I'm not going to impose mine on you. I've shared it here only to let you see my personal search for identity. Because that's what it was: a long journey, from my childhood into adulthood, to define myself, accept myself, and be loved for who I am. It's a journey we're all on, every last one of us.

So if you're gay, you're not mine to change—you're mine to love, appreciate, and point to Jesus, who knows you, loves you, and sees something wonderful in you. He alone has the right and the understanding to grow you, little by little, in every area of your life. But He won't do so in some harsh way that demands the impossible of you and then heaps shame and frustration on you when you fail. He's better than that, and he's got far better for you. The change he offers begins with a new identity that goes way, way deeper than a person's sexuality or anything else about them. It's an identity He gives to everyone who comes to Him, across the board—the identity and dignity of a beloved child. Like a loving and gracious mentor, He'll show you how to live out of that identity in practical ways rather than out of the countless false identities the world seeks to impose on all of us.

Society tells us, "Your activities determine who and what you are." It tells us that the way we feel must be the truth. And it tends to label people without examining their deeper circumstances. This is true regardless of how you, I, or any of us deal with our careers, our relationships, our sexual orientation, our education, our personal interests and pursuits—everything about us. It's a tactic of the Enemy. And it's why our core identity must come from Christ and Christ alone.

My husband is a great chef, and he made my wedding dress. Do these things make him a woman? No, they just mean he had a mom with great skills who taught her son. I love yoga pants. I could live in yoga pants. That doesn't make me a yoga expert. In fact, if I joined my husband's TruFusion class, in about five minutes I would be on the ground. Putting on yoga pants doesn't change who I really am. The same goes for the labels we put on ourselves. Identifying with something outside us doesn't change who we really are.

If you're an LGBTQ person and even these few thoughts of mine raise a red flag for you, then set them on the shelf. There's no judgment here. It's hard enough for me to work on my own issues. I would simply ask you to submit the broken areas of your life to God. Sexuality is an area of brokenness for everyone. We're all in it together, God is in it with us, and there's so much more to you, me, and all of us than just that.

Find the Purest of Gold

Scripture compares our faith to gold purified through a refining fire. In Zechariah 13:9, God says, "I will refine them like silver and test them like gold." To purify gold, you have to heat it to a certain degree and then scrape off the dross, or impurities. The quality of the gold depends on the amount of scraping. To get 14-karat gold, a little bit of scraping is required. To get 18-karat gold, more is required. And to get 24-karat gold, much more is required. Then to get platinum—the finest gold—the gold must be completely pure and rid of dross.

In the same way, we want to scrape impurities from our lives. We want to be the best we can possibly be. But to do that, some scraping is required. Getting rid of those impurities can be painful. It can sting. And in society today, we don't want to be uncomfortable. We don't want anyone to offend us. We don't want other people to say or think things different from what we say or think. The problem is that attitude doesn't allow us to become the best we can become. It doesn't allow for any scraping, so to speak. Scraping hurts. Scraping offends. But if we can't tolerate being offended by what people think, we can't grow or be purified.

There's a better way. We can start accepting that people do think differently from us. When things in our lives hurt, those scrapes are an opportunity to become refined, to become the purest gold we can possibly be.

Dear one, I pray for confidence in your identity. You are God's masterpiece. Whatever color your skin, whatever height your body, you are His masterpiece. Whatever you're holding on to as part of your identity, it's okay to let it go. God wants to expose your cracks so He can fill them with His purest of gold.

Reflection Questions

- What areas of your life do you feel inadequate in?
- Whom could you talk to about this so you can find freedom and healing? (Just think, I would still be a hairy beast if it weren't my friend talking to me.)

CHAPTER 9

EMBRACE THE SANCTITY OF LIFE

At nineteen, I got pregnant for the second time. During the first half of the pregnancy, all I knew was that I hadn't had a period for several months. I kept taking pregnancy tests, but they always came out negative. Then finally, after four months with no period, I decided to see a doctor to find out what was wrong.

"You're pregnant," he said.

"No, I'm not."

"You're one month pregnant."

"Well, if I am, I must be four months pregnant, since that's how long it's been since my last cycle."

"No, you're only one month pregnant."

I already had one child who was still in diapers, and the thought of having two children at my young age was overwhelming. Then this: If I was pregnant, I might not be able to dance. But my body was income.

Unable to handle it, I scheduled an appointment at Planned Parenthood. It would be just fine. After all, it was just a clump of cells, right? The abortion felt like something I had to do, not really an option. After all, this wasn't the first time I'd considered abortion. I got pregnant for the first time in high school. At seventeen, I was faced with choosing life or death for my baby. Terrified, I had no clue what to do. I talked it over with my mom, and she did the greatest thing any mother of a pregnant teen could do. She said, "I support your decision either way. If you choose to keep the baby, you can stay here, and I will help you raise your child."

With those words, she freed me. I knew I wasn't alone, that I had support no matter what I decided. However, even though I was terrified to do it, I liked the idea of raising a family.

Sweet Melissa was born one week after my eighteenth birthday, and I began the journey of being a mom.

Keeping Melissa was one of the best decisions of my life. But how could I even consider another child. This time, I was getting an abortion.

Then the night before my appointment, I had a dream. For some reason I was trying to care for not one but two babies, and I kept messing up because I didn't know how to manage it. But in the dream, I kept trying.

Oh my gosh, I thought after waking up. *This is a baby. This is not a clump of cells. It's a little life growing inside me. I can't do this.*

I called Planned Parenthood to cancel the appointment.

The guy I was with at the time was not happy with my decision, but I was determined that I would not end a life. I made another appointment with my doctor, and since I kept insisting I was four months pregnant, he scheduled an ultrasound right away.

"Oh, you're right," the ultrasound tech said. "You're four and a half months pregnant. And it's twins."

I didn't know God at the time, but through that dream, He not only showed me my sons' precious lives but spoke to my fears. I so desperately wanted to be a good mom, but I blew it all the time. We judge parents who are neglectful or addicts, but even when I was in those states, I really did want the best for my children. I just didn't know how to give it to them. But I am so thankful God guided me toward saving all their lives.

Amanda's Story

While at the strip club, I worked with a woman I'll call Amanda. She was one of the meanest, most aggressive women I had ever known. The day we met, she started our relationship by pushing me into a brick wall and explaining how she was going to beat my face in if I ever messed with her or her clients. With me in my four-foot-ten-inch body and her at least a foot taller, her behavior was quite intimidating. She bullied the entire club. Oh, and she did a significant amount of drugs.

One day, one of the women started to take some Valium from a bottle.

Amanda approached her. "Is that Valium?"

"Yes."

Amanda took the pill bottle out of her hands, poured out about six pills, and swallowed them all at once. Everybody was ready to call nine-one-one, but those pills didn't even faze her. She was someone nobody wanted to mess with, and nobody really wanted to talk to her either.

Before going out together one evening, a friend said she needed to pick something up. I thought nothing of it—until I found myself in Amanda's apartment.

I'm thinking, *Why on earth are we here?*

Inside, we sat down, and for some reason, Amanda told me about when she had an abortion. After the abortion was performed, her baby was crying—just a horrific cry.

Amanda sat up and said, "The baby's alive."

But the person performing the abortion said, "Yeah, but it will never live."

Amanda looked at me with the saddest eyes. "Then they picked up the baby and threw it in the trash can." It was a steel trash can, and she said she would never forget the sound of her baby's body crashing into the metal. The baby cried out in pain and just kept screaming. She begged them to help it, but they said, "No. It won't live." She was so distraught. She said it just ruined her.

Motherhood had never been in Amanda's plans; it was inconvenient for her, so she chose an abortion. But hearing her baby's cries destroyed her so much that all she wanted afterward was to be a mom. She went from never wanting a child to desperately longing for one. She wanted another chance.

So she got pregnant again. I can't recall if she married that man, but they did live together. She had the second baby and felt like her life was going to be okay. But when the baby was about two months old, the man, who was from a different country, wanted to take the baby to show it to his family. He did, and he never came back. For years, Amanda searched and searched and searched, but she could never find him or her child. That pain caused her much bitterness and anger, and when I met her, she was still living out the grief of losing two children.

What was supposed to empower her destroyed her. Society would say the freedom to choose gives women power, but that free choice ruined her.

Kaylie's Story

My massage gal, whom I'll call Kaylie, is wonderful, and I adore her. When she finally got pregnant after trying for a long time, she had an ultrasound that showed her baby had severe abnormalities. Her doctor told her the baby would not live—devastating news for any mom to hear. He recommended an abortion.

When she confided in me and asked what I thought, I encouraged her not to abort her baby. A decision no mom should ever have to be faced with.

The next time I saw her, I just had a feeling she'd had the abortion. When I asked if she had, she burst into tears, and I held her as she cried. Then I asked how she felt now that it was done.

"I hate it," she said. "When I committed to having the abortion, my doctor told me I had to go to an abortion clinic. But I didn't understand why I couldn't have the procedure done in the hospital. It was a medical procedure, right? My baby wasn't going to live. But they told me it was illegal to do abortions in a hospital."

Kaylie made an appointment at Planned Parenthood, and they warned her some people might be protesting outside the gates of their building. She was terrified to face them. But to her relief, no one was there that morning.

"The clinic was so cold and harsh," she told me. "Like, line 'em up, get the babies out, kick them out the door. It was horrific. There was no recovery time; I had to leave as soon as it was over."

She told me the worst of it was how both sides of the abortion issue reacted to her abortion. The pro-life crowd treated her like she was a murderer. She got zero compassion from them, even though she was grieving the loss of her desperately wanted baby girl. But the pro-choice people acted like it was no big deal. Just a cup of tea. Get an abortion, in and out, easy as grabbing a drink from Starbucks. Neither side would let her grieve.

But she did grieve even though she'd chosen the abortion. She'd longed for that pregnancy for years. She'd wanted that child. She chose the abortion only because she was assured the baby wouldn't live anyway. But she still felt the loss.

She asked the clinic staff if she could keep the baby to bury it, but they wouldn't let her. She told me she would always wonder what they did with her daughter. Why wouldn't they let her bury her?

Friends, this is such a sensitive topic, and I am totally pro-life, but it's so important to know how difficult a decision like this is. We don't know what people are going through. It's not our job to judge the situation. It's our job to love them through it.

I'm honored, grateful, and proud that Kaylie was willing and able to share this deep wound with us in hopes to help raise awareness and bring healing to others.

Confession at the Firepit

Mitch and I were leading a small group of young professionals when one of the women called us before our meeting. "I just want to warn you," she said. "My friend Allie [not her real name] is coming with me tonight. But she hates Christians, she hates wealthy people, and she hates conservatives."

"Fantastic," I said. "This is the perfect group for her."

Allie arrived, stepped inside our foyer, looked around, and then glared at me as if saying, *Yep, I've got you pegged.* Then she sat down in our living room and kept her arms crossed the entire first half of the meeting, still glaring at me.

She didn't know, but that week my sixteen-year-old boys had run away from home, and we'd had to place them in a lockdown boarding school facility in Utah. On top of that, I'd received the "How to Be a Better Parent 101" lecture from a friend (a mom who had only small children). But there I sat with thirty young professionals and shared my story. I was completely open about everything going on, and then I noticed a change in Allie. By the end of my story, she was bawling.

We were in the habit of giving our group real-life scenarios and then having them practice what they would say to encourage someone in that situation. We wanted them to always be ready to exhort, to be ready in season and out of season. So after I told them my story, I said, "Now tell me what you would say to me in this situation. How would you console me? How would you help me walk through this?" I shared how beat up I felt when people suggested I should have parented differently, and Mitch and I also talked about what can label and define us in life.

When I became a parent at barely eighteen, I was labeled a teen mom. I felt like everyone expected me to fail, and I had carried that insecurity my entire life, trying so hard to overcome it by being a good mom. Then when my boys rebelled and this friend lectured me about how I should have parented differently, it brought back every insecurity, every fear that I was failing as a mom.

Then we challenged the group with a homework assignment for that week, asking them to write down everything that labeled them and caused brokenness in them to expose the cracks so God could begin to mend those broken places.

The next week, Allie returned. This time we all sat around our firepit and, one by one, members of the group shared what they'd written. They didn't have to share everything they wrote, but they could tell us whatever they wanted. Then each person threw their paper into the fire.

After all the others had participated, Allie pulled out her paper and read it. But then when she was about to throw it into the fire, she pulled it back.

"I have one more thing to share," she said. "I had an abortion." She turned to the young woman who had invited her to our group. "It was two years ago, so my baby would be almost the exact same age as your little girl. When you had your baby, I was so sad I'd had the abortion. I still am. Every time I see your daughter, I see unfulfilled dreams, what might have been."

Watching Allie cry by the fireside, I could feel her pain. Those in favor of abortion talk about how having the choice to abort protects women, but I believe Allie's abortion devastated her. It broke her heart. By the time she finished sharing, every person around the fire was in tears.

When everyone was hanging out afterward, I pulled Allie aside and said I'd like to talk to her. Inside our house, I told her about the miscarriages I had before Zoë was born. I said, "You know, I was thinking. Maybe your baby ushered my babies into heaven."

She just wept and wept.

A few days later she sent me a card that said, "I want you to know I gave my life to Christ today. I hated Christians because of their judgment, and when you pulled me aside that night at the firepit, I was sure you were going to tell me I was no longer welcome in your group because what I had done was too horrible. And if you had done that, I would have accepted it. But when I told you my deepest, darkest story, you embraced me.

You loved me instead, and I'm a Christian today because of that love."

Now I was the one weeping. For me, losing a baby was worth it to have that moment when I could welcome someone into God's love.

What the Enemy intends for evil God turns into good. Since that time, I've had so many opportunities to talk about abortion, miscarriage, and the grief that comes with both. I wouldn't know how to relate to those experiences unless I had experienced something like them myself. As painful as the miscarriages were, I would go through them again. The fruit is worth the pain.

Embrace the Protection of Women Too

So much of the abortion conversation is about women's rights, but abortion crushes women. When a woman chooses to abort, it devastates her maternal instinct. God made us to be the mama bears, the fierce protectors of our children. We talk about rights for women's bodies, but what about rights for their hearts? So many women have no idea how much their abortion will damage them. They don't know until after the fact, when it's too late.

Save the baby, but save the woman too!

When I was pregnant as a teen, I chose to keep my babies, but I knew girls who'd had abortions. I fully supported the practice back then. Then with six miscarriages, I became well acquainted with the pain of losing a baby. Two times my doctor had to do a D and C to scrape out my uterus. Going under anesthesia knowing I'd wake up without a child in my womb was horrific.

One man equated the procedure to having a mole removed, and I was so offended by his lack of knowledge. A mole is merely a growth, not a human being. Removing it is drastically different from removing a baby from his or her mother's womb, and most people just don't understand how devastating the loss of a child is to a woman.

How can we as women terminate one life for the convenience of another life? Or even when, according to doctors, that life has little chance of survival after a full-term pregnancy when every child has value?

These days too many women say having an abortion was a great decision. Well, they're deceiving those who are unaware, but they're especially deceiving themselves. They can shout that idea to the world, but in secret moments, they'll wonder about the baby they aborted. *What would my baby have looked like? What would his first day of school have been like? What would have been her first trophy? Who would have been his first crush? Whom would she marry?* The burden is too much to carry, and it begins to affect them whether or not they realize it.

Those broken, shattered pieces tend to cut deep—until given the opportunity to heal.

We talk about women's empowerment, but abortion actually puts them in bondage. It does not empower women; it imprisons them with shame, guilt, and grief, and their silent suffering truly alters the course of their destinies. So my plea is for women who've come to realize the devastating effects an abortion has had on their lives to let their voices be heard. And even those of us who have not had abortions must speak up not only for the rights of the unborn but to protect women.

A Broken Nation

Can we admit we are a broken nation? We're bleeding at the seams. As of this writing, more than sixty million children have been aborted since the *Roe v. Wade* decision. Sixty million. That's more people that died in the Holocaust. That's more human beings killed than in any genocide in the history of the world. And God grieves.

In a broken society, silence equals approval. The citizens of Nazi Germany didn't approve of concentration camps, but they stood by silently and let them happen. Less than two hundred years ago, our society considered slavery an empowerment of the people. Oh, we felt sad about the way slave traders transported and sold slaves, and we said it was wrong for anyone to beat them, but we turned a blind eye to the truth. Only when people boldly stood up and said, "We see an injustice here, and it's wrong," did the practice of slavery change. Abolitionists not only fought for what they believed but died.

Margaret Sanger strongly believed in eugenics, and she saw birth control as a way to purify the population. (Eugenics is the same belief system the Nazis used to justify the Holocaust. It supports destroying a race or group of people considered inferior.) Here are a few excerpts from her writing and interviews:

"But for my view, I believe that there should be no more babies." (Among European women for the next ten years).[5]

"The most merciful thing that the large family does to one of its infant members is to kill it."[6]

"We do not want word to go out that we want to exterminate the Negro population."[7]

"I accepted an invitation to talk to the women's branch of the Ku Klux Klan. . . . I was escorted to the

5   Margaret Sanger, interview with John Parson, 1947, posted in Ben Johnson, "Chilling Unearthed Video: Planned Parenthood Founder Margaret Sanger Says, 'No More babies,'" Life Site, April 22, 2014, https://www.lifesitenews.com/news/video-planned-parenthood-founder-margaret-sanger-says-no-more-babies.
6   Margaret Sanger, *Woman and the New Race* (New York: Brentano's, 1920), chapter 5, "The Wickedness of Creating Large Families," accessed Dec. 30, 2019, http://www.bartleby.com/1013/.
7   Letter to Dr. Clarence J. Gamble, December 10, 1939, 2, https://libex.smith.edu/omeka/items/show/495.

platform, was introduced, and began to speak. . . . In the end, through simple illustrations I believed I had accomplished my purpose. A dozen invitations to speak to similar groups were proffered."[8]

"A marriage license shall in itself give husband and wife only the right to a common household and not the right to parenthood."[9]

"No woman shall have the legal right to bear a child, and no man shall have the right to become a father, without a permit for parenthood."[10]

"[T]hese two words [birth control] sum up our whole philosophy. . . . It means the release and cultivation of the better elements in our society, and the gradual suppression, elimination and eventual extinction, of defective stocks—those human weeds which threaten the blooming of the finest flowers of American civilization."[11]

Chilling stuff, right? Planned Parenthood has roots in the same philosophy that supported the Holocaust. Yikes.

---

8 Margaret Sanger, *Margaret Sanger: An Autobiography* (New York: Norton & Company, 1938) , 366.

9 Margaret Sanger, "America Needs a Code for Babies," *American Weekly*, March 27, 1934, typed draft article reprinted in *he Public Papers of Margaret Sanger*, accessed June 3, 2020, https://www.nyu.edu/projects/sanger/webedition/app/documents/show.php?sangerDoc=101807.xml.

10 Sanger, "Code for Babies."

11 Margaret Sanger, "High Lights in the History of Birth Control," Article 1, *The Thinker*, October 1923, 59–61, reprinted in *The Public Papers of Margaret Sanger*, accessed June 3, 2020, https://www.nyu.edu/projects/sanger/webedition/app/documents/show.php?sangerDoc=306641.xml.

Am I against abortion? Yes. I believe a baby in the womb should never be killed for the convenience of a mother or because of abnormalities. I believe each baby has value and a purpose.

What Can You Do?

The greatest call in society today is to end abortion. But we need to be willing to stand up and say, "This is not acceptable. I will fight for the voiceless. I will fight for those who cannot fight for themselves." We also need to stand united, and I truly believe that if we do, we can end this great genocide. But at the same time, we need to hear and understand the hearts of the people with whom we don't agree. If all we do is seek to be understood but never to understand, we'll have a further breakdown of society and more of the division we see in America now.

Today we're appalled by the Holocaust and slavery. Many of us are appalled by abortion. And I believe future generations will look back to this time when we killed our babies and wonder how we could have done so. After hearing Amanda's story about her aborted baby crying from that trash can, I think someone would have to be either completely naive or completely heartless to believe her baby wasn't a life. And knowing the devastation the abortion caused in Amanda's life, surely we must also think about the women who suffer.

Embrace the sanctity of life and do what you can to stand against abortion. At the same time, do what you can to honor and protect women and their God-given maternal instincts.

And for those of you who have chosen abortion, or will in the future, please know there is always hope. The broken places in us are the parts God makes the most beautiful.

Reflection Questions

- If you've had an abortion, there is healing, beloved. Talk to God about it. Ask Him to show you a safe person you can share with.
- Our nation is full of hurting women. How can you show love to women who have been affected by abortion?

CHAPTER 10

CONQUER THE IMPOSSIBLE

For Valentine's Day one year, Mitch surprised me with trapeze lessons. Since I used to be a gymnast and I love adventures, especially physically challenging adventures, my heart was exploding with excitement.

At the very first lesson, the instructor explained we were each to climb to the top of the ladder, where they'd harness us in and hold our waists as we leaned forward to grab the bar. Then the instructor would yell "Hep!" and let go, and we'd go flying through the air.

"I have three rules for you," he said. "First rule: Do exactly what I tell you. Second rule: Go exactly *when* I tell you. If you go prematurely, you won't be ready. If you go too late, you'll have missed your opportunity. Third rule: Just enjoy the ride."

Isn't that the way God is with us? All we have to do is listen to Him, do exactly what He says to do, then do it exactly when He says to do it and enjoy the ride. It's a beautiful journey.

When it was my turn, I started climbing the ladder toward the little platform about forty feet above the floor. Holy cow! Forty feet looks a lot more like eighty feet when you're on a ladder.

When I reached the platform, I saw that the girl waiting for me was even smaller than I was—and as I've mentioned before, I'm only four foot ten. She was probably in her twenties, but she was tiny. She hooked up my ropes, then grabbed hold of the harness around my waist. But I still hadn't let go of the ladder.

"It's okay, I've got you," she said.

I looked her up and down. *Whatever.* I wasn't trusting that little girl with my life. But to reach the bar, I had to let go of the ladder and lean forward. I had to put all my trust in this young girl holding me, or I would plummet and die (maybe). My heart pounded as I stretched forward.

I grabbed the bar and stood leaning at a 45-degree angle with this little girl holding my harness. Then the instructor yelled, "Hep!" and she let go. I leapt, flying through the air on the bar, dangling forty feet above the ground. It was so exhilarating, so beautiful.

Then the plan was to learn how to grab the arms of the guy on the opposite swing and let him carry you. We went through the same drill. I climbed the platform, then leapt from the top, holding the bar. While I was in the air, I swung my legs up and over the bar so I was hanging upside down by my knees. Then as I swung close to the other trapezes, I extended my arms. He grabbed them, and when I slid off my bar, he swung me through the air.

God really started speaking to me through this experience: *Your life is like this platform; it's your launchpad. To do something new, you have to let go of what's safe, what you've known. You have to trust that I've got you.* If we're going to follow God, we have to lean way out to where we would fall on our own if He weren't holding on to us. We have to lean, and we have to stretch, and we have to trust that God is always on the other end.

He is. He's got His arms out, and He's ready to catch you. But you have to let go of what's behind you to reach out for what's ahead of you. Life can be painful. The past has wounded us. Are we willing to let go of that pain to reach out for what God has in store? Yet we can feel uncertain: *Lord, I'm so far out here! If you don't catch me, I'm going to fall on my face.*

To trust God, sometimes the first step is learning to trust a person. I had to trust that the instructor knew what he was talking about. He was a real human being telling me, "Hep!" And that was a real person on the opposite trapeze asking me to reach out my arms and trust him to catch me. I also needed to be willing to let go of what I was holding on to. I couldn't grab what was in front of me without letting go of what had carried me to that point.

The House Story

In the Bible, the book of 1 Samuel tells the story of David, a young shepherd boy who defeated a giant. Conquering lions and bears threatening his sheep had given him the courage and practiced ability to battle the giant Goliath. By the time he faced Goliath, he'd learned to fearlessly trust that God could deliver his enemy into his hands.

Sometimes that's how God works. He gives us tests that lead to bigger and bigger trust.

God started putting it on our hearts that it was time to move. When we first started house hunting, I looked at one house and thought I felt the Lord saying, *This is the one.* But Mitch wasn't in agreement. I admit I tried to force the issue, but that resulted in an awkward situation. Let me just say we didn't buy that house.

It wasn't about the house, though. I could have moved into a trailer home and been as happy as could be. But I was confused because I thought God had been showing me that house was the one. Through that experience, however, I learned that even if I feel like God is leading me, my husband needs to be in agreement before I can move forward.

I also learned to be sensitive to the little details when God is closing doors. Sometimes we think what we're sensing is the will of God, but really it's just a lesson to prepare us for what's next. So that experience was my "lion."

We kept looking. In the meantime, God gave me a picture of our future house, the entire floor plan. I thought, *we're going to have to build this house because no house like this exists.*

He also gave me a mental picture of a room we'd have for a pastor's retreat, a room to welcome people from around the world. It was a large, spacious room with high ceilings, big windows with bright sunshine coming through, a door leading to a pool area, and a backyard with a stunning view of forested, rolling hills and mountains on the horizon. That confused me, because the largest room in the floor plan was the master bedroom, and if it was to be the pastor's retreat, how would we manage as a family?

Also, Mitch and I wanted a three-story house, but a room like that with a walk-out had to be in a basement. Basements don't have high ceilings. And they aren't well lit with big windows; they're dark. The layout simply didn't seem to work.

I said to God, *I don't get what that means.* But I wrote it all down and told Mitch what I'd seen. He thought

I was crazy, but then again, he knows I'm crazy. That was nothing new for him. I even started buying items for the pastor's retreat. For instance, if I was shopping and found furniture that would work, I purchased it, took off the tags, and stuck it in a box. I labeled the boxes "Pastor's Retreat" and stored them in the garage.

So there I was with all these boxes, thinking we would have to build the house I saw ourselves. All I knew was that we were supposed to have a pastor's retreat. We were supposed to use the house to welcome, house, and entertain people.

Then one day I saw a house online. As I looked through the photos of it, I thought, *This kind of seems like the same floor plan. That's really weird.* But the price was more than double what we could ever afford, and it had far more square feet than what I thought we needed. Still, I wanted to see what it looked like to get a feel for it.

I showed the house to Mitch and said, "What do you think of me just looking at this house?"

"Sure, no problem," he said. "But we're not buying."

"Of course. Definitely not buying it."

As soon as the realtor and I opened the big wooden front door and walked in, my heart started pounding. The foyer was spacious, and I could instantly imagine hosting crowds of people in the house. Then we went downstairs, and the ceilings were so high. The realtor said, "Yeah, it's kind of crazy. You're actually not allowed to have ceilings this high in basements, but the owner retrofitted the house to qualify as a commercial building so he could have that height in his office."

Then we walked down a long hallway, and at the end, a door opened into a large room, with the same high ceiling.

"This was the owner's office," he said. "It's the largest room in the house."

The room was bright and sunny, with windows on two of the walls. One of the windowed walls had a glass door that opened onto a beautifully landscaped patio and pool. Beyond the pool, the view was forest and hills as far as you could see, with purple mountain peaks outlining the horizon.

I came home laughing, I was so giddy. I couldn't imagine how we could afford the house, but I was learning to not trust my own judgment. I sat down and made a list of everything that would have to happen for us to purchase the house. It was a long list, and I wish I could remember everything on it. But, you know, they were just basic things like . . .

My husband had to be in agreement.

His income had to double.

Our current house had to sell within thirty days, but I didn't want to put it on the market until we moved out.

And—the final kicker—we'd have to sell a property we still owned in Utah.

That property was a house Mitch bought and renovated back when we lived in Utah. A friend who started a nursery and landscaping business asked us to partner him, and we did. However, then he injured his back, became addicted to pain medication, and started embezzling money. It was a horrible experience, and Mitch eventually had to close the business. But we never could sell the property. One winter, the pipes burst, and water flooded the main floor and destroyed everything on the ground level. We couldn't even give that house away. We didn't want to repair it, so it was just sitting there in Utah.

Well, technically we wouldn't have to sell that property to buy this house, I thought. I scratched that last item off the list.

Okay, God, I prayed, *if this is your will, then all these things have to happen.*

Facing the Bear

One day while Mitch was at work, I called him. "So, babe," I said, "let's just guesstimate. Speaking conservatively, how much would we need to put down on this house to have a healthy debt-to-income ratio?"

He threw out a number, and when I used an online loan calculator, the down payment was almost exactly what Mitch had guessed. He agreed that if we could afford the down payment, we should buy the house.

Number one, check.

Mitch is a partner at a software development company, and soon after that conversation, a potential high-end client completely outside of the box of normal operations started talking with them.

In the natural, this seemed like an impossible deal. However, Mitch is all about speaking life into situations! So he prayed hard, believed in faith, and worked his butt off.

Well, they were able to land the deal, and Mitch's income doubled.

Number two, check.

Mitch and I have learned that whenever we experience any financial increase, we need to ask God what He wants out of it, then listen for a specific amount to give. Well, before we even knew what Mitch's pay structure would look like, we sensed God telling us to give a specific amount—an amount higher than what we thought we *could* give.

"We don't even know if we'll have any money left over to put into the house," Mitch said. "We might even have to take money out of other resources to give God that much." But we decided to give the gift anyway and trust God to provide. Then we made a verbal offer on the house.

A few days later, I walked out to driveway and saw an envelope on one window of our car. It said Covenant Seed Blessing. Inside I found a check from some friends and a note saying "This is seed for your house. We believe in what you're doing."

Are you kidding me? It was a decent chunk of money, and I was shocked. Then as I was standing there in the driveway, envelope in hand, Mitch called me.

"They took another offer."

I pulled the phone away from my ear and looked at the phone. Then I looked at the check in my other hand. I looked at the phone again. I looked at the check again. Then I put the phone back to my ear.

"No, they didn't," I told him.

"Honey, they took another offer. The house is gone."

"You don't realize what's in my hand right now." I told Mitch about the check, the seed money for our house. "There's no way God would have told these people to give us money toward purchasing that home if buying it isn't the will of God. Mitch, this is our home."

I kept praying.

Then the owners of the house contacted our realtor. The other offer had been a cash deal from some people overseas, but after some hang-ups, the deal had expired. Now that same buyer was offering them a higher price, and they wanted to know if we would match it.

"No," we told our realtor. "God gave us the exact penny we're supposed to spend. We're not changing that."

The owners accepted the other buyer's offer, but the deal fell through again. Again the owners called our realtor, asking us for the higher price. But we kept saying no.

While these games were going on, God woke me in the middle of the night and said, *You shall love the Lord your God with all your heart, soul, mind, and strength.*

Yes, Lord, I prayed. *I love you with all my heart, soul, mind, and strength.*

I went back to sleep, and then He woke me again, saying, *You shall love the Lord your God with all your heart, soul, mind, and strength.*

Yes, Lord, I prayed a second time. *I love you with all my heart, soul, mind, and strength.* I thought maybe God wanted me to pray, so I prayed for a while, then fell back asleep.

God woke me a third time, saying the same thing. I got out of bed.

Okay, Lord. I'm up. What do you want me to know? I sat praying some more, and then I thought maybe He wanted me to look up the Scripture He'd been using. I looked up the passage in Deuteronomy 6 and started reading:

> You shall love the Lord your God with all your heart, with all your soul, and with all your strength. And these words which I command

you today shall be in your heart. You shall teach them diligently to your children, and shall talk of them when you sit in your house, when you walk by the way, when you lie down, and when you rise up. You shall bind them as a sign on your hand, and they shall be as frontlets between your eyes. You shall write them on the doorposts of your house and on your gates. (verses 5–9 NKJV)

I stopped at the part about doorposts.

That's funny, I thought. *We just talked as a family about the memorial stones we wanted to put on the doorstep of our future house.*

Then I looked at the word *gates*—plural. *Wow, the house has two gates around it.* I kept reading. Verses 10–11 said, "So it shall be, when the Lord your God brings you into the land of which He swore to your fathers, to Abraham, Isaac, and Jacob, to give you large and beautiful cities which you did not build, houses full of all good things, which you did not fill . . ."

Huh. The house we want to buy is fully furnished.

"Hewn-out wells which you did not dig . . ."

The property has three wells.

"Vineyards and olive trees which you did not plant . . ."

Beside the house is a full orchard bearing fruit every year. Oh, my goodness, this is our home.

If I hadn't been confident of that before, I was fully confident now.

We kept waiting, firm in our own offer, as offer after offer made to the owners failed to go through. For the seventh time (seven is the number of completion), one of the owners herself called to tell me they'd once again decided to take another offer.

This time I said, "That's fine. But *when* the offer doesn't go through, can you call me? Because we would like to buy your house."

Sure enough, several days later, she called again. The offer had fallen through, and she was willing to sell the house to us for the amount we wanted to pay.

"You have two weeks to close on this," she said.

Two weeks? We didn't have a loan, we didn't have approval on a loan, and we needed a jumbo loan, which takes longer than a regular loan. Even approval for a regular loan usually takes a minimum of thirty days. She had given us an absolutely impossible challenge.

But sure enough, by two weeks we had everything we needed. We bought the house and put our current house on the market. Now remember, it needed to sell within thirty days—item number three on my list.

We prayed about an asking price, then went to our realtor to put it on the market. Our realtor said, "There's no way you can sell your house for that. You're like $300,000 off."

"I know," I told him, "but this is the asking price God gave us."

"It won't even be appraised for that much. You cannot sell it for that price."

"I know, but it's the number God gave us."

He even drove me around and showed me similar houses, trying to prove I could not list a house like ours priced that high. But I still wouldn't budge. After all, it was the price God gave me.

"Okay, fine," he said. "I'll tell you what. You list it for whatever you want for the first thirty days. After that, if it hasn't sold, I can list it for whatever I want."

"Perfect," I said. Thirty days was my deal with God anyway.

Day twenty-nine. No offer, not even any interest. Really, nobody had even looked at the house. I started getting nervous.

It was March 5, and when I looked up my verse for the day, it was Joshua 3:5: "Joshua said to the people, 'Sanctify yourselves, for tomorrow the Lord will do wonders among you'" (NKJV).

I highlighted the verse in my Bible and then left it on the counter.

The next day, we finally had a viewing. The lady who came was a Christian, and she saw the verse highlighted in my Bible—the very Scripture she'd been believing for their next house.

"This is our home," she said. "We're buying it."

But our realtor was right; the house was appraised for a far lower amount than we were asking. Still, the woman had already made such a large down payment and wanted the house so badly that she didn't care. The bank approved her loan for the remainder of our asking price.

Number three, check. Again, I wish I could remember everything on that list! God did so many things.

The first day Mitch pulled up to our new house and began to weep before he could even type the code into the gate. He called our pastor, Pastor Don, and said, "I don't understand. Why doesn't everyone have a blessing like this?"

"Not everyone has the faith for it. Also, God knows what you will do with the house to bless others."

Mitch broke down again.

"God desires good gifts for His people," Pastor Don said. "Not that they need everything He gives them, but He wants them to know how much He wants to pour out His love and blessing on them and provide for them."

That really struck my husband. We believe part of the reason God gave us our home was to build faith in other people. As we share our story and welcome people into our home, we want to deposit in them faith and hope that God wants to do more in their lives. He can do abundantly more than anything they imagine. You see,

I really don't care about a house; I just want to please God. When we seek Him first, He will do more than we can ever comprehend.

Speaking of doing abundantly more, back to my list. I thought we had checked off all the items on it: Mitch and I were in agreement. His income had doubled. We had our dream house. Our old house had sold in thirty days. But God knew one more item should have been on the list, the one I crossed off too soon.

Two weeks after moving into our new house, I got a phone call from a woman in Utah.

"Hi," the caller said. "Do you own this house in Utah?" She gave the address.

"Yes, we do."

"My husband and I saw it when were out walking, and we just love it so much. But we looked in the windows when we realized it was vacant, and we noticed a lot of damage inside."

I agreed with their assessment. It was a lot.

"My husband and I love to renovate homes, though," she continued, "so we're wondering if you might let us live there rent free while we fix it up for you at no cost. Then maybe we could lease it from you to eventually own it."

Uh, are you kidding me? "Absolutely!" I told her.

A few months later, I got another phone call from her.

"We're so sorry," she said. "We really wanted to purchase this house from you, but my husband's parents aren't doing well, so we're moving back to the East Coast to take care of them. However, we have fixed up the house, and it looks fantastic, but we feel so bad about breaking our agreement that we'd like for you to keep everything we put in it." (You know, refrigerator and washer and dryer kind of stuff.)

They left behind a fully renovated, gorgeous house. We put it on the market, and it sold immediately. We never had to spend a penny.

Who does that? Imagine how much it must have cost them to renovate the house, and then they just left everything for us!

My list mattered to God. He took care of every detail, and He showed me how to walk in faith and trust Him fully. With the first house I saw, I tried to force a purchase in my own strength, and it didn't work. Then with the second house, I just let God be God and let go of my own desires. Instead of putting God in a box, I sat back to see what He would do. And He did exceedingly, abundantly above what we could ask, think, or imagine. I learned I could release everything to Him. I could, with His help, conquer the impossible.

So the first house was my lion. The second house was my bear. But I had yet to meet my Goliath.

Reflection Questions

- What do you need to let go of in order to grasp what is presented before you?
- What area is God asking you to just trust Him in?

CHAPTER 11

BE THE DIFFERENCE

Have you ever felt like you've finally begun to understand your purpose in life? Like everything that had happened to you and for you had been building up to that very moment in time? Well, that's what happened to me on a collision course with destiny on March 8, 2018.

Turn the car around, I heard God say.

What?

Turn the car around and go talk to that woman.

I turned my head, and there she was—a precious homeless woman sitting beside the road. Her name was Marie[12].

Now, let me back up for a moment. Mitch and I had taken a trip to Israel with the three founders of the Museum of the Bible, Steve and Jackie Green and Cary Summers. And as our group walked the land Jesus walked

---

12 Name changed to protect identity.

and came to an olive grove in the garden of Gethsemane, Cary told us about how resilient an olive tree is. If it catches fire and burns down, the sprouts still grow with new life. If it's cut down, it sprouts again. No matter how much that tree goes through, it survives.

Cary also told us about the process of making olive oil. The olives are brought to perfect ripeness, then crushed between two stones to bring out the oil. He told us how much of the oil comes from the flesh and how much comes from the seed itself. He told us about what it takes to extract the oil. And he told us about the different levels of oil. "The seed has such pure oil in it," he said.

Then he compared the olive to us. "A lot of Christians are used by God, and that's great." He paused. "But very few are willing to be crushed for the things of God." Then he so boldly asked, "What are you willing to be crushed for?"

Yes, Lord, I prayed. *Crush me. Do whatever you want to do in my life.*

Then Cary released the group to just walk around the garden of Gethsemane—the place where Jesus was betrayed so He could go and sacrifice His life for us—so we could pray and seek the Lord personally. I walked a little bit away from the group and sat down. Directly in front of me was the ugliest olive tree you could possibly find. I mean, it was ugly. It was mangled everywhere, and then just off to the side was this little branch that still had life in it. All around the ugly olive tree were gorgeous olive trees—healthy, leafy, and flourishing, with their golden-green leaves shimmering in the sunlight. But the mangled, pitiful tree in front of me had one branch hanging on for dear life.

I said to myself, *Wow, that's an ugly tree.*

And God said, *That's you.*

I'm an ugly olive tree? Thanks, God.

But as I thought about it, I realized this tree presented a beautiful picture. Through all the heartache and trials, there is still life. There is beauty in resilience. I took a photo of the olive tree and thought, *That's my tree.* It's still my favorite tree, and I can't wait to go back to see it.

Hebrews 5:7–8 says, "While Jesus was here on earth, he offered prayers and pleadings, with a loud cry and tears, to the one who could rescue him from death. And God heard his prayers because of his deep reverence for God. Even though Jesus was God's Son, he learned obedience from the things he suffered."

Jesus learned obedience through what He suffered. If we are to obey Him, we need to understand that we learn obedience through suffering too. What the Enemy means for evil, God uses for good. But for God to use it for good, we need to allow the suffering to create obedience in us. Ouch! I know. Yet the question isn't whether we're going to have trials. The question is how we're going to handle them.

That's right, treasured one. Suck it up, buttercup. Kick the devil in the head, release your trial to God, and let Him do some crazy good things in your life! After all, Jesus didn't *need* to learn obedience. He just needed to do it so we could understand that even Jesus, as both God and man, needed to operate with a spirit of obedience. Now we have no excuse.

Crush me, Lord.

Shortly after that garden prayer, I met Marie.

I was about to make some Kintsugi art for Zoë's class auction project. I knew I had all the supplies I needed, and I knew exactly where they were—in the third drawer down in front of the window in my kitchen. I pulled everything out but then realized the gold powder was missing. I searched the top two drawers, then the three drawers next to them. But it was nowhere to be found. So off I went to the craft store to buy some.

That's the day God said, *Turn the car around*, then *Go talk to that woman.*

After I turned the car around and pulled over, I got out and sat down beside her. Marie was homeless. All alone, sitting on the side of the road with a sign in her hand. I asked her how I could help, but I also asked her to tell me her story. We talked for about two hours, and I was blown away.

Marie had her first daughter at nineteen. I was eighteen when I had mine. Less than two years later, she had identical twin boys. Less than two years after my daughter was born, I had identical twin boys.

She was also a drug addict, abused, trafficked, and an alcoholic. And she was lost.

Her brokenness was so much like mine. At this point, I was kind of freaked out, and yet there was more.

One of her daughters was born without her esophageal flap developed. Well, now I was really freaked out. First, that's a pretty rare thing. Second, what a random bit of information to share. Third, *my* daughter was born without her esophageal flap fully developed. Okay, I was really freaked out at this point, I asked her, "What year were you born?"

She told me the year, and the month, and the day. It turned out that Marie was only nine days younger than me. I knew this was a God moment, and I went back to my car and began to weep. And still there's more.

As I cried out to God, He reminded me of a building with hundreds of dorm rooms that had been vacant for about five years. I thought, *how could this be? How could there be vacant buildings with all these homeless people?* The realization shocked me, and I went from ugly crying to just anger.

Then I was so graciously reminded of a Bible study I had led two days prior, where I was literally pointing my finger at people saying, "You go be the difference you want to see in the world. Quit whining about it. Quit complaining about it. You go be the difference." And I sat there clearing my throat, still in shock, saying, *Um, God? You want me to be the difference?*

I was sure I clearly heard Him say people like Marie need four things: they need Jesus, they need someone to believe in them, they need training and education, and they need opportunity.

Still in my car, I said, *Yes, Lord, I will do it. Whatever it takes.*

After composing myself, I headed to the craft store and bought the gold powder. When I got back home, I set it on my countertop—about six inches away from the gold powder I had been looking for! I began to weep again. God had set me up. He really wanted me to meet Marie.

Isn't it amazing that I met her on a trip to purchase gold powder to create Kintsugi art? Truly, God had turned the cracked places in my life into gold, enabling me to help women and children in need. This encounter was the inspiration that led to the creation of Providence Heights.

Marie turned out to be an unusual case. She actually preferred living off the grid to housing options. I did my best to help her and her kids while respecting her choice, and when she moved to a different state, we stayed in touch through text messaging until the number I had for her ceased to work. She is a precious woman, and she is constantly on my heart.

Meeting Goliath—Providence Heights

If I look at those first two houses as my bear and lion, then Providence Heights is my Goliath. We're working on purchasing a hotel as a future training center, where we'll house women and children in need, providing counseling, education, and jobs. It will be a place of hope and restoration.

But most importantly, we want Providence Heights to help women discover their identity in Christ. And we won't call our building a *shelter*. What might that word speak to the people we serve? *You've failed. You've come to the end.* No, Providence Heights is a *training center*. That term says, *This is your place of opportunity and growth. Your launchpad. The place where your desires and dreams begin to unfold.*

Same space. Different perspective. Training and support give people an opportunity for a beautiful future and a hope. And if God cares about where I live, how much more does He care about where hundreds of women and children in need live?

One day, after a particularly discouraging conversation about this project, I came home feeling like I had been kicked in the gut. I went to my room to worship God, pray, and process what had just happened. I was standing by my window, looking at the view, when God whispered, *Remember where you're standing.*

I looked at my bedroom floor. God was right. He had brought about the purchase of this house when it seemed impossible, and the very floor on which I stood was a sign of his faithfulness and promises. It doesn't matter what I see in the natural. I just need to trust Him and remember His promise.

God told me, *This is not going to happen the way you think it's going to happen, so don't try to put me in a box.* Then He reminded me of a ski trip Mitch had taken with his family in Montana.

The first day, it was super foggy. All the kids really wanted to go skiing, though, so his parents decided to let them. Mitch's mom skied with them, and they had a blast. The next day, this one perfectly sunny, they went back up the mountain to ski again.

Mitch's mom looked down the mountain and said, "Oh, my gosh, I am not going down that."

The kids all laughed and said, "But this is the exact same mountain you skied down yesterday."

"Yeah. But I had no idea what it looked like." She literally sat on her butt and slid down the mountain.

As Mitch's mom shared her story, God spoke to me: *That's what I do with you. If I show you the whole picture, you can't handle it. You would slide on your butt all the way down, missing your opportunity. Instead, I say, "Can you go this far, honey? Good job!" And then "How about a little bit more? That's awesome." Then, "A little more, baby girl? You've got this." And before you know it, you've made it down the mountain.*

As I stood in my bedroom praying, God reminded me of that lesson. He saw the whole picture, but all I needed to do was focus on what was right in front of me.

Providence Heights is a mountain of a project, and that day it felt huge and overwhelming. I felt a sense of responsibility for the thousands of women who could stay there, but I was so afraid of falling, of being crushed. Then I felt the Lord saying, *Just focus on what's in front of you.*

In this world of uncertainty, it's easy to put pressure on ourselves, certain we need to figure everything out. But Jesus Christ, the Messiah, mediates for us. He intercedes on our behalf. We just need to go to Him and trust Him. We can let go, learn obedience through what we suffer, and trust that though it might feel like we're falling, good will result from the struggle.

Being Inconvenienced

Our sweet miracle daughter Ariel got married in 2017, and she wanted to have the wedding in our backyard. Not only that, she wanted the ceremony to be on the island in our pond. Trouble was, the "island" was just a mound of dirt covered with blackberry bushes. We had to build an actual island and a bridge to it.

Earlier that spring, we had taken on a new stockbroker. Mitch didn't know him very well on a personal level, but the broker would call Mitch every so often just to let him know the status of our funds and about the investments he was making on our behalf.

As they were talking one day, Mitch sensed something was off, so he asked him how he was.

"I'm good," he said, no doubt assuming the question was just common courtesy.

"No, how are you?" Mitch asked again.

"Well, I'm not very good," he said, admitting the truth. "I was just diagnosed with cancer. I have only a few months to live."

Before long he was in the hospital. Mitch knew he didn't believe in God, so he decided to visit him even though he didn't have time to do it. We were building that island and bridge as well as installing a waterfall feature in the front yard, and the wedding was only weeks away. We were all working like crazy. But Mitch just felt he had to visit our broker—and more than once, even though the hospital was an hour and a half away. Mitch would drive the distance just to spend time with this man whom he didn't really know.

As the broker reached the end of his life, he told Mitch his wife had always wanted to raise their daughter in the church. But he'd never allowed it.

"What do I need to do?" he asked. "I'm afraid to die."

Mitch walked him through a prayer of accepting Christ, then told him what heaven would be like, which comforted him.

Then the man asked, "What can I do for my family?"

"The greatest thing you can do is tell them you've received Jesus and that you'll be waiting for them in heaven."

We can all come up with reasons not to help someone. The question isn't whether helping is inconvenient; it's whether we're willing to be inconvenienced. If we're going to walk in obedience to God, the reward for inconvenience is great. Because Mitch was willing to be inconvenienced, one more soul is in heaven.

I often think back on my prayer time in the olive grove and Cary Summers's question: "What are you willing to be crushed for?"

After a particularly stressful day working on Providence Heights, I said to Mitch, "I did not sign up for this."

Mitch just laughed. "Oh, yes, you did."

He was right. After listening to Cary Summers speak in Gethsemane, we started praying for God to do something crazy good in our lives. He's been faithful to do that.

Looking at my life today, I can see that every circumstance has culminated in preparing me for Providence Heights. All the heartache, all the brokenness, all the skill sets I thought were insignificant—all of it has prepared me for such a time as this. I feel called. I feel a burden.

This is not where Mitch and I pictured we would be at this stage in life. We were getting comfortable. Mitch and I could have chosen to just step back and start coasting. But then God laid Providence Heights on our hearts.

As I look back over everything I've endured in my past, I know I would experience it all again in a heartbeat. Every heartache. Every moment of suffering. If I would have the chance to help set other women free, it would still be worth it. All of it.

Precious one, God has a plan for the brokenness in your life, a plan to restore you, heal you, and empower you. He glues the broken back together with gold so we can enter into others' pain and show them He is their gold too. So we can be the difference.

We are strongest where we've been shattered, and our brokenness is what makes us beautiful.

Reflection Questions

- Have you prayed for God to crush you?
- Are you willing for Him to answer that prayer?
- What are you willing to be crushed for?

A PRAYER
FOR YOU

Dear God,

We are all broken in some way, and I pray that all the precious women who have traveled this journey of trial and triumph with me in these pages would find victory in their lives, and that You would take their broken vessels and make them new. Take those shattered areas in their lives and make them whole again, Lord.

I pray, Father, for whatever areas they have felt brokenness in, that as You mend them stronger than gold, they would be able to use their lives for Your glory, love others, and take what the Enemy means for evil and turn it for good. I pray that You would set the captives free. We are more than conquerors through Christ; we are overcomers! I pray for victory, victory, victory in the life of every mighty warrior.

And, God, if any person reading these words doesn't know You as their loving Savior, I pray that they would take a moment now to ask You into their heart, just as I did so many years ago.

In Jesus' mighty name, amen.

LET'S CONNECT

I would be so honored if you would like to reach out and connect. I would love to hear your story or how this book has impacted you.

Ways to connect:
Phone: 425-753-5856
Website: ChristineSoule.com
Website: providenceheights.org
Email: christine@providenceheights.org

All of the proceeds from this book will be donated to Providence Heights, a Christian nonprofit 501 c 3, organization that provides housing for women and children in need as well as counseling, education, and jobs.